TITTER YE NOT!

William Hall, currently Presn critic for *Prima* magazine, ha five years, specializing in sh

He first encountered Frankie Howerd when out of the blue he received a letter thanking him for a review in the *London Evening News*, where he was film editor for twenty-one years. That was a quarter of a century ago and over the next twenty-five years he interviewed the comedian on numerous occasions.

As a biographer and scriptwriter his published works include *Raising Caine*, the authorized biography of Michael Caine, and assisting Norman Wisdom in the autobiography *Don't Laugh at Me*.

William Hall lives with his wife Jean, son Will and daughter Juliette in Highgate Village, North London.

For Jeannie, Will, Juliette and Lena
with my gratitude for their inspiration,
support, and their patience.

WILLIAM HALL

Titter Ye Not!

The Life of Frankie Howerd

Grafton

An Imprint of HarperCollins*Publishers*

Grafton
An imprint of HarperCollins*Publishers*
77–85 Fulham Palace Road,
Hammersmith, London W6 8JB

A Grafton Original 1992
9 8 7 6 5 4 3 2 1

The acknowledgements on p. 187 constitute
an extension of this copyright page

A catalogue record for this book is
available from the British Library

ISBN 0 586 21773 8

Set in Times by Avocet Typesetters, Bicester, Oxon

Printed in Great Britain by
HarperCollinsManufacturing Glasgow

RESEARCH ASSISTANT
Juliette Hall

Special thanks to:

Bobby Jaye

Lew Lane

Mike Maloney

Jacquie Kavanagh, Jeff Walden
and the Staff at the BBC's
Written Archive Centre, Caversham

. . . and to all Frankie's many friends
and fellow entertainers who contributed
to this book.

Without whom . . .

Contents

Foreword by Peter Rogers   9

Preface   13

1   Early Days   15
2   Early Signs   24
3   Basic Training   33
4   On the Road   44
5   Radio Waves   56
6   Sunny Interlude   69
7   The Spice of Life   80
8   The Other Women . . .   90
9   Ups and Downs   103
10   . . . And The Other Men   120
11   Carry On   127
12   Bottoms Up!   143
13   In The Wars   163
14   Fond Farewell   171

Epilogue   182
Filmography   184
Acknowledgements   187

Foreword
by Peter Rogers

It is easy to make unkind remarks about people. The very thought of them sometimes inspires bitchery that could rival Oscar Wilde or Noel Coward. But when it comes to saying kind things you find yourself at a loss for words, new words, words that haven't been said before.

That is how I think of Frankie Howerd, how everybody I know thinks of him. What can you say about such a person? It was impossible not to like him. It wasn't that magic ingredient misnamed Charm, the sort of thing usually associated with motorcar salesmen. Charm in Frankie would have been suspect. In fact, you could almost say that he was so completely lacking in charm that he actually charmed you. He grew on you, like friendly moss. You could never tire of his company because he was never aggressive or pushy. He didn't talk about himself all the time as other actors do. He was a patient listener and always gave you the impression that he was interested in you and what you had to say. He made you feel wanted, possibly because that was how he felt himself. He, too, wanted to be wanted.

Professionally, he was a Master. He was the original Deliberate Mistake. No pause or hesitation in his act was unrehearsed or not carefully considered, and he had that gift of making you feel embarrassed for him as he walked up and down the stage looking as though he didn't know what to say next. But he knew exactly what he was going to say next and exactly when. It was a very cunningly contrived ruse and quite original. And it worked every time. It was the most successful con trick of all time and every time it came off you admired the perpetrator more.

The most heartening and heart-breaking of Frankie's appearances was the occasion when he appeared before the Oxford Union. It did your heart good to see the old trouper playing with such a young and critical audience and holding them in the palm of his hand. They loved him and he could do what he liked with them. I think that on this occasion if he had just stood on the stage saying nothing they would have loved him still because that's what he was — someone to love.

In my own experience I know that I always looked forward to the day when Frankie was due on the set at Pinewood. I enjoyed watching him perform and I enjoyed meeting and sitting with him off-set. He never asked you what you thought of his performance, not because he wasn't interested but, as was so natural to the man, he did not like to ask. To him such a thing was bad manners. And if you did praise his performance he would simply say: 'You think so? Oh, good.' It wasn't said dismissively. He cherished your opinion, but didn't want to be effusive. To him that would have appeared insincere.

It is a pity to have to talk about Frankie in the past tense. When I heard the news of his death I swore, as you would swear if you dropped your ice cream on your foot. That doesn't mean to say that Frankie was no more important than a blob of ice cream. It means that his death was unnecessary. It seemed all wrong, a mistake, and I almost expected to hear that it was untrue, a rumour. Sadly, it was true and always will be. And that is the greatest pity of all. That dear amicable man is not here now and we notice the loss because he was so rare.

'A comedian need not necessarily be a humorous person. Indeed those who have been most successful in exciting laughter have often been men with a disposition towards melancholy.'
DOCTOR SAMUEL JOHNSON (1709–1784)

'Oh titter ye not. No, listen. *Lis-sen!* Everyone is being very tittersome tonight.'
FRANKIE HOWERD (1917–1992)

Preface

His letter came out of the blue.

It landed on my desk on a breezy March morning in 1966 as I stood by the window of the *London Evening News* looking down on the bright yellow vans parked the length of Tudor Street, just another envelope in the batch of morning mail.

Except that this one was different.

The address was badly typed, and unevenly spaced. But inside was an unsolicited letter from a comic I had found side-achingly funny, even when I wasn't all that sure exactly why. Frankie Howerd had always made me laugh, usually in fits and starts and abrupt bellows rather than prolonged mirth. He had that quality of surprise that kept you on tenterhooks for the next line even as he jollied you along on some impossible foray into his own misadventures.

I had reviewed *The Great St Trinian's Train Robbery* for the paper, and liked what I saw of Frankie amid the flying gymslips and stocking-tops of the little horrors of Ronald Searle's warped imagination. The letter of thanks that he sent me was a reflection of the man who wrote it, with an appealing honesty, a heart-warming naïvety of sorts, to which you couldn't help but respond.

We met numerous times after that, usually in his dressing-room after a first night with the congratulations flowing, but also in his London homes. And amid the uncertainty and self-doubt that plagued him, just as it does every great comedian, you could sense the warmth of someone who needed to be wanted – or was it the other way around?

It was this warmth that came through and touched the hearts as well as the funny-bones of millions, capturing a whole new generation of young people in his later years. It made Frankie's passing all the sadder when it happened.

But this book is mainly about the fun times, the ludicrous moments, the paradox of a man who brought laughter to millions yet too often for his own good was a soul in torment.

A complex, fascinating figure whose like we will never see again. I hope you enjoy meeting him.

WILLIAM HALL
London, August 1992

1

Early Days

The first memory Frankie Howerd could ever recall was falling downstairs as a toddler and landing on his head, thus uttering the first '*Oooh . . . aaah!*' of the many that in later life would bring laughter to millions the world over.

He was almost two years old at the time, and it happened in the terraced house at No. 53, Hartoft Street, York, close to the City Hospital where he was born on 6 March 1917. It was young Frankie's first bruising encounter with a world that would batter his emotions and his ego, turn him into a hypochondriac – yet provide the basis for a humour that in its own uniqueness will never be equalled.

At the start, who would ever have guessed it? His father Frank Howard – Frankie later changed the spelling – was a soldier, Private No. 6759 in the 1st Royal Dragoons, while his mother Edith worked in the Rowntree chocolate factory in the city.

Edith was petite, slim, with black curly hair that hinted at her Celtic background – she had a strict Scots Presbyterian upbringing – and possessed an appealing, almost soulful look that her eldest son would inherit and eventually exploit to its fullest advantage.

The portents were intriguing. Plotting his chart, Royal astrologer Penny Thornton would find that this particular Pisces with its Moon rising in Leo, a pronounced Jupiter, and Uranus and Mars in an opposing position to the Sun would all mean . . . that Francis was in for a rough old time.

'He would be a born actor, sentimental, moody, volatile, quirky and acerbic. And predisposed to a certain irreverence and rebellion against authority,' she asserted. All of which would prove to be spot on.

But at that point all he had was a headache. It was six months after the tumble that Francis Alick Howard, a lusty infant with a strong pair of lungs, was taken south with the family when his father was transferred to the Royal Artillery, promoted to

15

sergeant, and posted to Woolwich. The family moved into a house at No. 19, Arbroath Road, Eltham, a terraced street in the poorer part of the area, much of it long since pulled down to make way for a housing estate on that faceless fringe of South London.

But in those days there was space, and plenty of it. Green fields, trees, hedgerows abundant with wild life, and a view that stretched away towards the Weald of Kent. The house had a large garden with a lot of lawn, and young Frankie grew up amid the greenery, playing happily for hours in the grass, inventing jungle games and becoming adept at climbing trees. Those early days would leave their mark on him, creating a fondness for the countryside that never left him.

Who else do you know who regularly rehearses his lines in front of a cud-chewing audience of cows? Frankie would go on to do just that, and describe them as highly appreciative of his talents.

But for now he was a chubby child with fair hair like his dad − Tennyson might have been writing about him when he penned: 'Shine out, little head, sunning o'er with golden curls . . .'

Money was scarce in those early days after World War I, and the family were poor without being destitute. Sergeant Howard was based six miles away in the Woolwich Barracks, headquarters of the Royal Artillery alongside the imposing Royal Arsenal, founded by Henry VII, that took up a mile of choice Thames skyline on the south bank. Even though he would arrive home most weekends with the weekly pay packet, it was left to Edith to feed three mouths as well as her own − Frankie's younger brother Sidney had come along, and a year after that his sister Betty was born. Frankie himself, who remained a bachelor all his life, always said he had a church named after him at his own christening: 'York Spinster!'

Growing up into a tall and gangling lad, he saw relatively little of his father, and even less when Sergeant Howard was invalided out of the Royal Artillery and transferred to the Education Corps to supervise the academic training of young soldiers around the country.

His father was diagnosed as having a hole in his lung − brought on, like so many of his comrades, by the dreaded gas swirling around the trenches of Passchendaele in Belgium − another statistic of the War to End All Wars.

Frankie and his dad were never close, whereas he was his mum's darling, and remained so until her death in 1962 at the age of sixtynine. In fact, his father's prolonged absences created a palpable tension in the family whenever Sergeant Howard reappeared out of the blue for a few days' leave, and the barrier between him and his young son became insurmountable. 'I positively resented his intrusion,' Frankie would reveal later.

On one memorable occasion his parents did take him on a rare family night out — into the smoky interior of the local working men's club, where little Francis, aged four, was given his first stab at fame: to go on stage, sing a song, and come away with a bag of sweets as a prize.

Frankie's reaction? 'I howled the place down. I was absolutely petrified, and struggled and screamed blue bloody murder to get off. But I still got the bag of sweets!' He could have had no idea then, but it was the shape of things to come.

Stage fright would stalk Frankie for the whole of his career, often leaving him quivering in the wings or in his dressing-room, numb with terror, steeling himself to walk out and face the public gaze.

Growing up amid the rural Nine Fields of Eltham — a village, incidentally, that spawned another comic son in the shape of Bob Hope — young Francis found himself increasingly retreating into a solitary world of dreams and fantasy. He would go for long walks alone, creating his own scenarios like any imaginative young boy — but with a difference. His dreams took him out in front of applauding masses, bestriding the stage like a colossus, master of the theatrical manor and all he surveyed. At the age of ten he was even practising how to sign his autograph.

The Howard children went to the local Gordon Elementary School, named after the hero of Khartoum, where Frankie proved a model pupil, anxious to please. So much so that on his first summer holiday when the school was set a mathematics task of three hundred sums to solve over the long nine weeks off, studious Francis was the only pupil to struggle through the lot. Mathematics was his best subject, geography his worst.

His mother's Presbyterian background ensured that her eldest son was enrolled for Sunday School almost as soon as he was tall enough to reach the door handle of the church hall at nearby St Barnabas.

Frankie found himself instinctively drawn into this friendly, dedicated new family with all the security it represented. It was his first taste of religion and he became addicted to it.

In next to no time he had eagerly signed on for the Band of Hope and the Society for the Propagation of the Gospel. Plus the local Cub Scouts, even though the weekly vow of 'Akela, we promise to do our best' made little impression on him – Frankie was, and remained, hopeless in anything of a practical nature.

Eagerly, Frankie would look forward to the Sunday School annual treat, a church outing to Herne Bay. The family were too poor to afford proper holidays, apart from a single week in Brighton for Mum and the three children when school packed up for the summer.

Edith Howard did her best with precious little in the kitty and Frankie could recall a magical evening when he was first taken to the pantomime: Boxing Day 1925, aged seven, to 'oooh' and 'aaah' at the romantic tribulations of another dreamer, *Cinderella* no less, at the Royal Artillery Theatre, Woolwich. His mum took her brood along on the bus to join the Boxing Night throng for the cheap seats in the gallery. They queued for two hours for the 8.00 p.m. performance – but Frankie, cheering Nora Delaney as Prince Charming and booing the Ugly Sisters for all his little lungs were worth, treasured the memory all his life.

Thirty years later he would step on to that same stage for his own show, and be surprised at how small it was. At the age of seven, it looked huge.

'I was hypnotized by the fairyland magic, a world in which everything was beautiful and glamorous,' he would recall. 'It was an exciting, glittering, over-the-rainbow world, and I wanted to become a part of it.'

The Boxing Night panto became a treasured annual date in the Howard diary. At home, Edith Howard encouraged her young son to create his own tiny wonderland in the front room: a tea tray for a stage, rags on sticks as makeshift curtains, actors cut out from cartoon drawings and pasted on cardboard so that they could stand up. Then Frankie would invent his own stories, shifting them around the stage as he talked his way through their adventures for hours on end.

He never tired of it, and at weekends after Sunday lunch he would put on special performances for his mother, brother and small sister.

Now Frankie's mother was forced to go out and do charring for wealthy families on the 'other' side of town to make up the money to support her own family. She scrubbed floors, washed dishes, cleaned rooms for a few precious pounds. But the kids never went hungry or found themselves without clean clothes. The pride of a working-class mum saw to that.

By coincidence, it was at this time that the eager-beaver young Francis decided to embark on his first commercial venture to make himself a spot of pocket money. He persuaded the little girl next door, a winsome moppet named Ivy Smith, to help him mount a concert party — and charge admission.

Their stage was the end of the garden, with the fence as backcloth. The time was Saturday afternoon. The audience — asked to fork out a farthing for the privilege — were the local neighbourhood kids. And the wardrobe belonged to Frankie's mother and Ivy's parents, who knew nothing about it. Draped in clothes several sizes too big, the pair paraded around giving full rein to the imagination of their youthful entrepreneur—producer.

Until Mum finally appeared on the scene, took one look at her clothes being dragged across the grass, and demanded: 'What's going on here?'

Frankie proudly informed her that he was giving a concert — and, what's more, making money out of it. The reply was a sound cuff around his head, and a stern lecture from his mother along the lines of daylight robbery, ending with the order: 'Give it all back — now!'

A chastened Francis surrendered his profits and, rubbing his head, reflected that show business had its pitfalls after all.

Scholastically, Frankie Howard was nobody's fool. At the age of eleven he sat for the entrance examination to Woolwich County School for Boys, later to become Shooters Hill Grammar School

– and won a scholarship there. He was awarded one of only two London County Council Scholarships that were on offer.

On 1 May 1928 he duly donned a smart uniform of blue blazer, grey trousers and black tie with gold stripes, and set off across the fields for the daily 45-minute slog to a brand new school. Young Francis Howard walked into the new building in Red Lion Lane with four hundred other children of varying ages and abilities, sharing the tummy-butterflies and usual mixture of anticipation and trepidation on the first day of any term. Frankie, trudging along the footpaths that morning, was in a blue funk at the prospect of being in an alien class – socially as well as academically.

Shooters Hill Grammar was a mixed fee-paying school that drew its pupils from a wide circle of well-to-do middle-class families embracing Greenwich, Blackheath and south as far as Bromley. Today it has changed its name to Eaglesfield, and with 1,500 pupils is the largest secondary modern boys' school in southern England. But in those days, as a scholarship boy Francis stood out in a smaller crowd, or felt he did, and the knowledge did nothing to help his innate shyness and over-sensitivity.

But he was tall for his age, though thin as a rake, athletic, and proved good at sport. In a school where cold baths and cricket counted for everything, sporting prowess was the green light to popularity, and soon he was accepted by the others and indeed became a leader on the field of human conflict where willow meets leather.

Even at that age, he had a long reach and large hands, and became a demon bowler for his team.

A slight hiccup came in his first summer term when he was smitten with a young girl in his class, and made the mistake of writing her a love letter, which he tentatively passed to her under the desk. 'Her name was Sheila, and I had a huge crush on her.' Such is calf love – but some cad got hold of the precious missive, and next day it appeared pinned up on the school notice board for all the world to see. 'Oh, the shame of it!' Frankie would wail later, still squirming at the memory of the hoots of derision before he elbowed his way through the crowd and tore it down. But he got his own back the following Saturday by taking six wickets in six balls, and was hoisted shoulder high by his team-mates to be carried off the field in triumph.

Working hard and playing hard, Frankie's schooldays were days he could look back on with pleasure and not a little nostalgia. He joined the school dramatic society, and immediately made his mark as a leading light on the boards. He even turned his hand to writing short plays, and submitted *Lord Halliday's Birthday Party* for a school concert. But the headmaster, Mr Rupert Affleck MA, studied the hour-long script and found that his tastes and those of his thespian pupil didn't quite tally.

He banned it.

Undeterred, Frankie was in every show that came along, eventually earning himself the nickname 'The Actor', a flag he waved with enormous pride. If those childish plays improvised at the bottom of his garden were the seeds of what lay ahead, the school concerts were the first flowerings which suggested that perhaps his destiny lay in the theatre after all. Instinctively he felt drawn to things artistic.

He also contributed to the school's annual magazine. *The Ship* was an impressive piece of work, a bound volume of more than one hundred pages detailing the exploits of the boys and girls — and, most important, of their prowess on the sporting field of battle. Reports of house matches between Brodie, Briggs, Leather, Clark and Platt — named after the housemasters who ran them — took up many pages.

But so did the pupils' own efforts, and no second guess needed for who set out a page of jokes under the headline *Howlers* in the 1932 issue . . . They were typical schoolboy humour, as bad as any you will find in any school magazine anywhere — but in Frankie's case, an early taste of things to come.

Sample: *Ali Baba means being somewhere else when the crime was committed.* (Think about it.)

> *Poll tax is a tax on parrots.*
> *People go around Venice in gorgonzolas.*
> *A senator is half-man and half-horse.*

They don't write scripts like that now — or maybe they do.

Shortly after this minor triumph, a school health check was less successful. On Frankie's medical card of 25 October 1932 appeared two rather ominous words: 'Back stoop.' It was the first sign in his teens of a condition that would plague him on and off for the rest of his days.

Meantime, something else that would become a lifetime's odyssey – and eventually a soul-searching dilemma – took over in a big way. Every night the young Francis faithfully went down on his knees by his bedside and said his prayers. He kept a Bible by his bedside, and read it last thing at night before switching the light out.

On Sunday he went to the church of St Barnabas on the corner. And at the age of thirteen he was deemed knowledgeable enough by the church elders and the Revd Jonathan Chisholm, vicar of St Barnabas, to be invited to become a Sunday School teacher. On Monday evenings he joined half a dozen other tutors from the diocese at the vicar's home in Appleton Road for tea and cakes, and instruction for the following Sunday's work.

Problem: Francis was not a good listener, and his attention was inclined to wander into the dream clouds as the vicar droned on. Result: when it came to the class on Sunday and he was facing a dozen eager young faces in his room off the church hall, he had no idea at all what he should be telling them.

But never one to be lost for words, Francis – he never quite made it to St Francis, though he admitted to it as a fleeting thought – launched into great yarns from his imagination featuring pirates, detectives and historical adventures.

In those days the face that would later launch a thousand quips – and virtually never veer from the script on TV, stage, screen or radio – proved a dab hand at off-the-cuff invention. Like the story-tellers of old, Frankie entranced his youthful audience – and the word spread. This was the room to be in. He received the plaudits from the Revd Chisholm with due humility, even if the Bible had taken a back pew that day. Luckily the vicar never sat in. He even encouraged his young protégé to join the Church Dramatic Society.

But now, at thirteen, a crisis loomed. The signs had probably been there, along with the growing pains of a shy introvert lad who longed to proclaim his talent to the outside world. Suddenly young Francis developed a stammer, a genuine speech impediment he put down to a mixture of wanting to please and over-eagerness to get the words out. 'I was all stutter and gabble,' is how he summed it up.

Also looming on the horizon was a church performance of *Tilly of Bloomsbury*, a vintage comedy by Ian Hay, and Francis practically went down on his knees to beg them to let him take part.

Enter Mrs Winifred Young – one of the several women who Frankie would later claim unequivocally to have had a major influence on his life, and the direction it took. Mrs Young was the producer, and she saw something in the shy, stumbling youth beyond a stutter and a capacity for walking into the scenery.

She found a role for him – Tilly's father, aged all of sixty-five, complete with false beard, who would stalk around the stage declaring his faith in his daughter's virtue through his whiskers. Mrs Young took the embryo actor under her wing, inviting him round to her house in Westmount Road on Tuesday and Thursday evenings, and laboriously rehearsing him for two hours in the subtleties of enunciation and, above all, talking s-l-o-w-l-y.

And she won through. Slowly Francis relaxed, learned to enjoy his lines, forgot his nerves in the concentration on the part. 'She was my Professor Higgins,' he said. 'I did exactly what she told me – and when it finally happened I was the hit of the night!'

He was, too. The unwieldy youth whose features were ill-disguised behind a long grey beard won the loudest applause. More important, he even won a few lines in the local paper's review. The *South London Press* singled him out for praise, and Francis proudly cut out the six-inch critique and pasted it in a school exercise book.

'It was my first Press cutting,' he recalled. 'But I had to wait a precious long time for the second!'

2

Early Signs

Someone had said something to Frankie that took root inside his head and wouldn't let go.

It happened as the curtain rang down in St Barnabas Church Hall on the last ripple of applause for *Tilly*, and a sweating potential star-is-born unclipped the spectacle frames that held his beard in place and breathed a deep sigh of relief.

'You know,' said the someone, 'you should be an actor . . .'

Frankie never remembered who owned the voice. All he did know was that a gangling thirteen-year-old who had taken three curtain calls owed that someone a debt of gratitude. Because those lucky seven words welded a sudden determination inside him, turned the crossroads sign round from religion to acting – though some say pounding a pulpit isn't that much different – and sent him on his way with a swing in his stride.

Suddenly Frankie Howerd knew, with incontrovertible certainty, where he was heading.

'I could so easily have gone into the Church,' he said. 'I had religion instilled into me from the day I was born.'

His mother had been at the play. When he went home that night and told her of his Big Decision, Edith Howard, bless her, gave him a hug and said: 'That sounds like a nice idea, Francis.' It may have been the euphoria of the moment, or she may have been following a mother's instinct of knowing when to agree with your offspring's wildest dreams, but for Frankie it was the seal of approval he needed.

Frankie sensed her true feelings, but said nothing. 'I think Mum was disappointed that I decided against entering the Church,' he told friends later. 'But thank God she supported me all the way. If she had come down heavily on me, I don't know what I'd have done.' Luckily, Mum was too sensible.

The next day Frankie enrolled for acting lessons.

His father was home, but doing very little to help. Finally invalided out of the Army, he took a local job as a clerk, but the pay was so poor that his wife still had to keep scrubbing the floors and polishing the furniture to make ends meet. In that year, 1933, the sixteen-year-old Frankie had little idea what was going on outside the unremarkable but comfortable confines of Eltham. The only clue was in the line of grey-faced men he would pass in the dole queue stretching round the block outside the local labour exchange.

The world was a bitter place, and that spring saw the height of the Great Depression with three million unemployed and the average manual wage standing at £2.10s. (£2.50) a week.

The sprawling tentacles of suburbia were reaching out from London, slowly but remorselessly grasping the precious green acres of fields and hedgerows and slipping them into its hungry concrete jaws. Ironically, given the economic climate, this was the year of the first housing estates, with building hitting a record for the century and new houses going up at the rate of a thousand a day, selling for £350 each, with a down payment of just £5 to clinch the deal.

All Francis saw of the emergence of a brave new world was the tearful face of his beloved mum when his brother Sidney and sister Betty had to be taken away from school at the age of fourteen. His parents could no longer afford their education. The youngsters were shunted out into the big wide world – Sidney joined the Post Office as a clerk, while Betty found a job as an office junior. Francis, resting on the laurels of his scholarship, stayed at school. 'Quite honestly,' he admitted later, 'I never had any idea of the sacrifices my parents made to keep me.'

A year later it would just be his mum. After his father died in 1934 it was she who refused to give in. Instead she worked herself to the bone to keep the family intact. It would be a mixture of guilt and affection that kept Frankie close to her for the whole of her life. When fame and fortune came, he never forgot the early days and what she did for him.

But right now his mind was on rather more than academia. The London County Council, or LCC, ran evening classes for aspiring actors, and that included all aspects of theatrical work. Frankie enrolled, and after a few months with the LCC Dramatic Society was told of a chance to be promoted to the acting heights – to

RADA, otherwise known as the prestigious Royal Academy of Dramatic Art. Or, if you prefer, mecca to every young hopeful in the land. The Academy was floating its own scholarship around like a tempting carrot.

Frankie's teacher at that time was an actress named Mary Hope, who would seem to have had more faith in her pupil than he did in himself, and put him to work in prolonged coaching sessions. The examination required the embryonic thespians to spout an extract from a contemporary play, followed by two Shakespearian soliloquies. Frankie stifled his nerves, and agreed to take the plunge.

On a dismal grey day he set off from home in his best suit, clutching a packet of cheese sandwiches his mum had made him for lunch. Frankie got off the train at Holborn, and walked the half-mile to No. 62, Gower Street, where the imposing RADA building is located. He had been jittery to start with, the butterflies in his stomach fluttering with growing urgency as he got nearer to his goal. Walking through the doors, he would say, turned him into a 'near wreck'.

He records what happened next in graphic detail.

'I shuffled into a vast room where the other candidates were waiting, and was summoned in for the audition, absently clutching my sandwiches. That's when my nerve went. My left leg started to shake — the original knee-trembler! Then I started the speech.

' "*To be . . . um . . . er . . . to be or . . . um . . . n-n-not to b-b-be . . . Th-th-that is . . . is . . . is . . . um . . . er . . . the quest-quest-question . . .*"

'That's when my bag of sandwiches burst, showering crumbs and cheese all over the floor . . .'

Poor demoralized Frankie squeaked his way through the audition, knowing from the expressions of the three judges that he was on a hiding to nothing. He stumbled out of the audition room, shouldered through the crowd waiting their turn, and fled into the cold grey afternoon.

Well aware of the sacrifices his mother had made, Frankie felt he had failed her. 'I had let everybody down. My mother, the school headmaster, my mates, my tutor, everyone. And myself. On the train home I just stared blankly out of the window. But when I got to Eltham I couldn't bear to face her.' He found himself in a field at the back of the house — 'where I sat in the long grass, sobbing my heart out.'

The tears dried. Frankie Howerd sat there for two long hours. And slowly his mind cleared.

'I had a strange premonition,' he would describe it later. 'Call it a flash of intuition — call it anything. But I sat bolt upright in the grass, and said aloud: "*You're stupid!* What are you? Plain stupid! God gave you a talent, and if it's not to be an actor — what then?'

'And the answer came: a *comedian*!

'Why not? I didn't have anything to lose, except my pride — and that was wounded enough already after such a traumatic day.'

Frankie crawled home at sunset to face his mother, and break the bad news to her. When she heard about the RADA débâcle she smiled sympathetically, patted his shoulder, and gave him a kiss on the cheek. When she heard about his new ambition to be a funnyman, there was the briefest of pauses before she nodded and said: 'If it makes you happy. As long as you're kind and decent, I don't care what you do.' What more could a devoted son ask of a devoted mother?

Frankie left school. He had no great diplomas to his name when he shook hands with the headmaster and turned his back on the gates of Shooters Hill Grammar for the last time. Just a GCE (the General Certificate of Education). His name is listed under the farewell *Valete* in the 1935 school magazine.

But he had some good memories to take away with him — and he'd managed to filch the cricket ball with which he took the six-out-of-six to become a hero for a day.

Now it was time to get a job, and help with the family finances. In those hard times it was anything but easy, but after prodigious scouting of the area Frankie landed a job as a filing clerk with the firm of Henry A. Lane, Provisions and Produce, at No. 37—45, Tooley Street in the East End — at the princely wage of £1 per week. The job was dreary and dead-end, the only relief being after work when Francis found solace in Southwark Cathedral, where he would sit alone in a pew for hours listening to organ music or concerts — and on one unforgettable occasion

the St Matthew Passion which seemed to scorch its way into his
very soul.

His religious zeal burned as vividly as ever, coupled with a
growing appreciation of music. 'I know nothing about classical
music,' he confessed once. 'But it all adds up, doesn't it?'

As he shifted restlessly at his desk overlooking the docks,
Frankie's pen toyed with shipping orders and invoices while his
mind was elsewhere – in the realm of the theatre, and the local
concert parties around Shooters Hill where once more he was a
leading light. His boss didn't help. According to Frankie, the
manager – one Henry Lane himself – had a limp, a black patch
over one eye, and a malevolent gleam in the other, a legacy from
the Great War. Mr Lane vented his spleen daily on the hapless
youth in his charge – and Frankie, being Frankie, was panicked
into making ludicrous mistakes like spilling tea in the boss's lap
or ink over the desk.

In the ten weeks he worked there, Frankie also came out in an
unsightly rash of boils, caused by a mixture of stress and being
run down. They were the first of innumerable ailments which
would dog his footsteps over the ensuing years, earning him his
unfortunate reputation for hypochondria, much of it well-
founded. But to start with it was just boils.

The final straw in Frankie's unhappy association with the
company came when a bundle of documents he dispatched to
Vladivostock was opened and revealed to be a programme for
a revue he had just put on called *Frank Howard's Gertchers
Concert Party*. It was a case of 'Kindly leave the office' – and
Frankie, at nineteen, found himself enduring the humiliation of
the dole queue for the first time in his young life.

His mother helped find him his next job. The head of the
household where Edith Howard did her daily cleaning chores ran
an insurance company, heard about her son's sorry tale, and gave
him a post as a clerk in the firm's Southwark office at thirty
shillings a week.

But by now all Frankie's creative juices were flowing into his
amateur dramatics, with concert parties taking up most of his
energy. That meant comedy – and he worked day and night to
think up sketches and routines he could perform in the local

church hall, old folks' homes and even for the Shooters Hill Dramatic Society he had joined. He formed 'Frank Howard's Knockouts', insisting once again that his name was in the title — the first significant traces of a performer's ego becoming apparent?

Travelling to concert dates could prove a problem, but Frankie was nothing if not an opportunist, and thumbed a lift with anyone who would take him. Once he found himself on the back of a motor bike *en route* home after the annual Herne Bay Sunday School outing. It poured with rain. The upshot: to boils, add pneumonia.

Frankie expanded his concerts to other boroughs, and was soon performing in church halls throughout South London — and all for free. He even changed his name to Ronnie Ordex for a time, decided he didn't like it, and changed it back again. Finally he felt it was time his efforts yielded a material dividend.

He started looking around for a suitable place to air his talent — for money. His first tentative attempts to turn professional resulted in dismal failure. But the boy tried, how he tried! Now twenty-one, he wrote himself a comic monologue, and rehearsed it until he was word perfect with scarcely a hint of a stutter. Then he thumbed through the entertainment columns to find the nearest music hall that was featuring what he was looking for. Talent Night!

In the thirties most of the country's music halls put on a 'Friday Night is Talent Night' spot in their bill at one time or another. All Frankie had to do was pick the theatre, make his way there, and join the queue to put his name down on the list. He made sure he came on early so that he didn't have to wait around too long kicking his heels and trying to control his nerves. That first monologue failed to get the laughs, so Frankie ditched it. The following week he put on schoolboy shorts and tried out a comic song. Again, a smattering of applause that sounded suspiciously like sympathy. Next, he switched to impressions. James Cagney, Charles Laughton, Noel Coward, they all came in for their share of mimicry. The trouble was that they all sounded the same. Frankie wrote that off to experience, and went back to playing safe — telling jokes.

It was at the Lewisham Hippodrome that he decided to try

the one about Long John Silver and Jim Hawkins . . .

Long John is standing by the rail staring out to sea when Jim
tentatively approaches him and plucks at his sleeve. 'Yes, lad,'
growls the old sea dog. 'What be ye wantin'?'

'I was wonderin', Long John,' ventures young Jim, 'how you
come to lose your leg?'

'Aaargh, that come from a cannon fired from a Spanish ship.
I'm walkin' the deck when — whoosh! This cannon ball takes
me leg clean off. But quick as a flash me mates find a piece o'
wood and screw it in — and I'm as good as new.'

'And . . . how come you got a steel hook for a hand?' queries
young Jim.

'That, lad, be when I'm fightin' Bluebeard the Pirate. He gets
in a lucky swipe with his cutlass — and me hand drops overboard
into the sea. Quick as a flash me mates grab a steel hook from
the deck and screw it in — and there it is! Good as new.'

'Finally,' pursues the lad, 'that eye patch. How come you're
blind in one eye?'

'Ah that! That's seagull droppin's!'

'But seagull droppin's don't make you blind — '

'It do', says Long John [and here Frankie would crook one
finger at his eye] 'if you've got a hook for a hand . . .'

He should have stayed in bed that day. On the bill were comedians
Jimmy James and Derek Roy, both of whom had their own highly
individual line in comedy patter, so the audacious tenderfoot
found himself in tough company, while Jack Payne and his Band
kept the music swinging. Jimmy — real name James Casey —
was perfecting the drunk act that would be hailed as the best of
its kind in comic history. As he staggered on in top hat and tails,
trying to reach the cigarette in his mouth with two wavering
fingers, you could almost see the stage tilting beneath him as he
attempted to stay upright. He would become known as 'the
comedian's comedian', and Frankie, watching open-mouthed
from the wings, could never have guessed that within twenty years
he would be following his idol out on to the stage of the London
Palladium in successive Royal Variety shows. Or that Jack Payne
would one day become his agent.

'Jimmy performed his drunk act like a rhythmic ballet. There was a kind of beauty about it,' Frankie said, marvelling. 'Humour is all about conflicting elements – and here was a drunk performing a ballet! There's conflict for you.'

Derek Roy was making lesser waves, but would go on to become the resident comedian on the BBC's *Variety Bandbox*, the most successful radio show of its kind, and Frankie would join him in presenting the show on alternate weeks. *A-mazing* – but that night in Lewisham his career could have been nipped in the bud for all time when he suffered the ultimate humiliation for any comic . . . being hooted off the stage.

New talent went on right after the interval. Jimmy James had closed the first half, and curiously enough excelled naturally in the style which Frankie would later adopt. He was a brilliant adlibber, and could milk laughs from the slightest chance remark. He was once asked by a BBC producer what he did on the stage, and replied: 'I'm glad you brought that up. It's been worrying me for years!' While in a historic live radio show from the Garrick Theatre in the early fifties he mislaid his script and went through an entire nine-minute sketch with a bemused Tony Hancock as his feed, making it all up as he went along. And nine minutes can be a long time.

Curtain up. Frankie heard his name called. Taking his usual deep breath to stem his nerves he walked out with as much confidence as he could muster – and froze as a blinding spotlight pinned him to the stage like a fly in aspic. He gulped, tried to stammer out the start of the Long John Silver story. And dried.

Someone in the audience tittered.

Frankie tried again. After a few seconds his voice faded away into silence. The huge theatre was deathly quiet, suddenly hostile.

And poor, unfortunate Frankie just stood there, the shivering hub of his own personal nightmare.

'I had never known anything like it – and yet it was what I'd wanted all my life,' he said much later, appreciating the irony of that dreadful night. 'I could only stand there like an idiot screwing up my eyes against the glare. I tried to get going on the joke, but it was so off-putting that my voice just tailed away and I dried up! I suppose I just wasn't used to it.'

The audience started to laugh and heckle. Boos and cat-calls mingled with the jeers. From the pit the orchestra leader hissed, 'Say something — or get off the stage!'

Frankie got off the stage. His eyes were streaming with tears of humiliation.

It was a chastening experience, the kind where a brave soul might say to himself: 'One day I'll laugh about this . . .' And he did, years later, with Derek Roy. But not then. Frankie turned up his coat collar and crept away into the night.

He tried again, this time with the Carroll Levis Discoveries — nothing to do with jeans — that would eventually become a hit TV talent-spotting show. He keyed himself up no fewer than four times. 'Comedy, impressions, comic monologues, dramatic speeches, I tried them all.' Result? 'Nothing. It was no good.'

Successful amateur, failed pro. Frankie Howard's *curriculum vitae* could have been summed up in those few words, and it hardly made impressive reading. He could make people laugh with his sketches and gags on a local level — church hall audiences loved him. But when it came to the 'real thing', as far as a career in comedy was concerned, he was up against a brick wall and he knew it. Worse, he could see no way round or over it.

Then the war came, and with it a chance to conquer fresh pastures. That's if he could conquer his nerves first.

3

Basic Training

Five months after war was declared on 3 September 1939, Frankie received his call-up papers. Why the War Office waited until February 1940 before deciding that Howard F.A. should do his bit for King and Country has never been made clear. As it turned out, for the first two years of his service he lived up to his initials, and did just that.

He applied to join his dad's old regiment, and was duly accepted for the Royal Artillery. First stop: the barracks at Shoeburyness where they fitted out his tall, ungainly figure in khaki, found him a bunk in one of the dormitory huts, and set about turning the new recruit into a fighting soldier.

Of course, it was hopeless from the start. Frankie was willing, no doubt about that. But his innate nervousness led him into all sorts of scrapes, the kind that would not be out of place in one of the *Carry On* farces he would later adorn.

First, basic training. It was nerves, he insisted, that led him to answer back to the fearsome Sergeant Major Alfred Tonks at his first appearance on the parade ground. To actually mutter the words '*Speak up!*' when the sarge was bellowing his guts out in a roar that scattered the pigeons, smacked suspiciously of potential suicide rather than a wish to see the war through.

From that moment Private Howard's fate was sealed. He was singled out as a troublemaker, and paid the price accordingly.

A fellow recruit, Private Peter Enright, recalled the early days of square-bashing with a nostalgic smile. 'They had us out there all day and every day trying to drill some kind of discipline into us. But poor old Frank just couldn't get it together. When the sarge shouted "Right wheel!" once, Frank actually headed off to the left. And when the order came to "Mark time!" − guess who bumped into my back and sent me sprawling into the bloke in front? Right first time.'

It was worse when it came to weaponry. After his initial introduction to the heavy .303 Lee-Enfield rifle, Frankie knew they were not destined to be friends. As someone who never got beyond the primary school level in Do-It-Yourself – his later boast was that he couldn't even change a light bulb, let alone a fuse – Frankie was as out of place stripping down a rifle as a car mechanic performing a heart transplant.

Sergeant Major Tonks dubbed him the 'Unknown Quantity', and made his life a misery. But the one thing Frankie did know about himself was his desire to get back on the boards.

'I couldn't help myself. Even while I was square-bashing on the parade ground I was day-dreaming about it. Performing was something that was absolutely compulsive, and I must have had some sort of innate belief in myself to flounder on,' he would claim later.

At that point in his life he needed all the faith in himself that he could muster. The Lewisham débâcle had been the start of the first low point in a career that would see him soar to the heights of stardom and sink to the depths of despair. But that was for later. Right now, if there was a graph on the wall of Frankie's personal profit-and-loss account, it would show a minor dip.

His ego had been further dented on the actual outbreak of war, when he immediately applied to ENSA (Entertainments National Services Association) to offer his own services. 'I wasn't trying to dodge the column,' he stated later. Just trying to do what he thought he was best at – entertaining.

Frankie's best wasn't good enough. He found himself alone on the vast stage of the Theatre Royal, Drury Lane, which was frightening enough in itself, auditioning in front of an Army major and a group of colleagues, all of them in uniform. Years later he would hold that stage, and a 2,000-strong packed house, in the palm of his hand. Right then, gawky and uncertain at twenty-two, the sight of the khaki-clad line-up in the fourth row was too much.

Maybe it was a combination of the brooding atmosphere of the huge auditorium and the gaze of the critical authority. But once again his 'nervous tendency to go to pieces at the wrong moment' – Frankie's own words – got the better of him.

The message was: Thanks a lot, but no thanks. Frankie gave them a weak salute, and found himself out on the street.

But now, at last, came his chance to shine. If not at the Front

– well, at the back. The rigours of square-bashing day after day over the hard Tarmac at Shoeburyness were behind him, a memory of wasted hours and sore feet. He was transferred away from the basilisk stare and frightening lung power of Sergeant Major Tonks to B Battery in another section of the barracks, accorded the rank of Gunner, and taught the rudiments of the British Army's fire-power in the face of a forthcoming Nazi invasion.

Because the threat was very real. The ill-fated British Expeditionary Force on the beaches of France had its back to the Channel, and the little boats prepared to sail for Dunkirk. All leave was cancelled. France was about to fall. From the safety of the garrison walls on the north bank of the Thames Estuary, Gunner Howard watched the small craft edge past the Maplin sandbanks on their way from Canvey Island, Westcliff and Southend to brave the *Luftwaffe* dive-bombers and write their own page into history.

And he waited for the call.

Which never came.

Instead he whiled away the hours until a different, unexpected demand came through: the urgent need in these darkest of hours to boost morale and give the chaps some diversion. In other words, camp entertainment. Frankie would prove adept at that, in every sense.

He stepped forward smartish, offered his services as a comic, and was snapped up on the spot by a grateful Entertainments Officer, possibly because there wasn't too much other noticeable talent around at that time. At the first Sunday night concert in the Mess, he was introduced as 'Gunner Frankie Howard' – another first, because up to then he had always been called Frank. Away from the footlights he would remain Frank to his friends and relatives, Frankie to the profession.

'I didn't like Frankie too much,' he admitted later. 'It seemed positively babyish.' But to the regiment he became Frankie, and to his comrades that's how he stayed.

He went down a treat. Officers and lower ranks alike guffawed and cheered at his jokes. The Lewisham Hippodrome faded into obscurity.

*

The memory of those early days watching the North Sea stayed with him forever, to be recalled whenever the talk returned to 'What did you do in the war . . . ?'

He remembered the sandbags along the beachfront at Southend, with Gunner Howard stretched out face downwards in their protective shadow, toes and elbows digging into the sand, peering along his rifle barrel through the barbed wire at a grey horizon with palpitating heart, waiting for an invisible enemy to appear. Frankie always likened it to that scene in the war epic *The Longest Day* when the helmeted German manning a pillbox on the coast of France saw the D-Day armada emerging out of the mist. 'I knew how he felt. I think I'd have had a fit if that had happened to us.'

It didn't. There was no German armada, just rumours.

Frankie told a nice story about how he and a young Welsh rookie were seconded to guard Wakering, a village not much more than a speck on the map located on the Essex marshes below Foulness Island. Actually there is a Great Wakering and its sister hamlet of Little Wakering, and it was their duty to ensure the two hundred-odd residents slept peacefully at night, knowing the British Army was on hand to protect them.

In fact the British Army consisted of Frankie, Dai and a tent in which they took turns to sleep while the other stood guard on round-the-clock twelve-hour shifts. In that summer of 1940 Frankie would clump around the country lanes, with his rifle in his hand and ideas for comedy sketches churning in his mind.

Back in the tent they had set up with a local farmer's permission in a secluded corner of a turnip field, he would jot down the gags and save them for — who knew when?

One day the farmer emerged from his gate to accost Frankie in the lane. 'You know, son, we're really grateful to you,' he said.

'Oh?' said Frankie. 'Why's that, then?'

'Well, we can hear your boots marching up and down, and it gives us a great sense of security. If there is an invasion — we know you're there!'

Yes, thought Frankie. Me and my rifle and ten rounds of ammunition to hold back the hordes. He thanked the farmer, and stomped on down the road, extra loud.

In fact, it was an idyllic time – and idle. If there was a war on, he wouldn't have known it, apart from the blackout curtains over the windows of the farmhouses and the occasional plane flying overhead. Otherwise, in that hot dry summer, the only sounds to disturb his train of thought were the tractors in the fields and the cheery hum of insects in the hedgerows.

It was with mixed feelings that Gunner Howard was ordered back to the garrison as the first chill breath of autumn filtered through the trees. Sorry to leave the friends he had made in the village. Glad to have another crack at the concert parties and try out his new material.

Back at base, Frankie was swift to approach the Entertainments Officer. His enthusiasm proved infectious and soon he was practically running the weekly shows single-handed.

'Tact', he admitted, 'was never my strong point. I tend to speak my mind.' And speak it he did, with increasing volume and acerbity as the Sunday nights drew nearer and nerves started fraying. 'There weren't too many comedians around, so I largely had the field to myself. Just as well, because I wanted – nay, Francis, *insisted* – on being top of the bill!'

His rivals for the place of honour were usually singers, both from the Royal Artillery and the women ATS, who would help vary the bill, plus an assortment of conjurors, musical maestros, jugglers, even dancers. But Frankie was already virtually a semi-pro, head and shoulders above the rest, and he could pull rank on them all – in expertise if not in authority.

Insisting on anything in the Army when you are a lowly gunner may seem out of step with reality. But with a cunning combination of 'Francis at his most charming' and friendly persuasion, plus his sheer talent for making people laugh, Frankie invariably found himself where he felt he belonged. Top of the programme, closing the show. And always to the clamour of cheers, clapping and boot-stamping that are music to a performer's ears. Particularly to one with a swollen head.

Because Frankie *was* cocksure, and he didn't mind who knew it. 'Yes, I was arrogant,' he would admit. 'I thought I knew it all. I mean, I felt some of them weren't out of short trousers when it came to performing.'

The weekly Music Hall was a kind of military 'Sunday Night is Talent Night'. Now, for the first time, Frankie was not afraid to exploit his nervous stammer. He found it got laughs, and began to capitalize on it.

First step: get the audience on your side. Frankie did this by the simple method of creating a conspiracy with his listeners. 'Rather than acting *to* them, I did it *with* them. I told them my misfortunes as if I was gossiping over the garden fence. It's the sort of thing you hear any night in any pub in the country. Everything happened to me, except that I let it get completely out of hand, and carried it to extremes.

'It worked because people identified with my troubles. There but for the grace of God . . .

'I was a bit raw in those days. But the essence of my act was born there, the seeds were sown in that Army camp on Sunday nights in the Mess.'

In the crowded, smoky haze with the troops crammed at tables over their beer, Frankie hit the right nerve — and touched funny-bones. The other secret of his act was that everything he did tilted at Authority — with a capital A.

Later he would christen all bosses, be they managing directors, chief producers, entrepreneurs or impresarios (take a bow, Bernard Delfont!) with the sobriquet of 'Thing'. For now his barbs were directed at 'Them', the faceless Top Brass who were never named but shown up as causing Gunner Howard F.A. maximum discomfort while sheltering behind their pips and their stripes. He would end his act for the troops by leading them into one of the wartime songs that brought a catch to the throat and a tear to the eye: 'White Cliffs of Dover' or the rousing 'Bless 'Em All'.

Frankie's face was rapidly becoming his fortune in terms of the laughter it provoked. So was a voice which had the first hint of what later persuaded Harry Secombe to suggest he wore 'the tenor's friend — a truss with a spike in it.' It could be likened, as one critic suggested, to 'A corncrake suffering from an overdose of gravel'.

In fact Frankie had been working assiduously on his voice while on lonely patrol in the country lanes of Essex. He told his friend Lew Lane, the producer of numerous events for the Water Rats charity, how he expanded his vocal cords. 'I sing the alphabet,' he revealed. 'It's really very simple.' And in front of Lew one night in his dressing-room at the Prince of Wales Theatre he sang it from A to Z, up and down the scale.

'They say some actors can read a telephone book and make you laugh,' Lew said later. 'Hearing Frankie sing the alphabet sent shivers down my spine. All the letters had a resonance of their own . . . it was weird.'

Weird or not, it worked. Frankie grew in confidence. And his voice grew fuller by the day, its range reaching out to the corners of the low-ceilinged Mess at Shoeburyness Barracks.

He totally flouted the advice once given to budding comics by the legendary Lupino Lane: 'Any inclination to fidget and lack stage repose should be immediately controlled. This can often cause great annoyance to the audience and result in a point being missed. Bad, too, is the continual use of phrases such as "You see? . . . You know! . . . Of course . . ." '

But on an unashamed wave of 'You sees' and 'You knows' emanating from the makeshift stage by the bar, no one could possibly miss the rumpled khaki-clad figure fidgeting and pulling faces up there through the cigarette smoke.

'Listen . . . *Lis-sen!*' it exhorted. The voice was demanding, petulant, and in the end it got its way. *'Pull yourselves together! You'll make me a laughing stock, you know. Now, who can manage a little titter? It isn't always easy to get your titters out on a wet Sunday . . .'*

They listened. They got their titters out. And they laughed.

Full of new-found zest, buoyed by the applause of his weekly ventures on to the public stage, Frankie grew bolder. His sister Betty helped out on some occasions, forging the close-knit bond that would stay with them for life. Sometimes he persuaded her to take to the stage as his stooge, even sing a song or two. At other times she would take the train out from Fenchurch Street on a cheap-day return to lend him moral support.

Frankie's downfall came one November day in 1941, and it was spectacular.

Autumnal mists were swirling around the barracks, lending a chill to the air from the North Sea. To cheer up the battalion,

Frankie persuaded his Entertainments Officer to put on a lunchtime show in the Mess.

Only this time he was in drag.

'I was dressed as an old ATS scrubber, with huge balloons pushed under my jacket, a straw wig, a white powder face and a great half-moon blob of lipstick over my mouth,' Frankie would say, regaling friends with the story after much persuasion. 'I got up on a table and sang a comic song − but in the middle of it, the air-raid siren suddenly started up.

'Everyone stampeded for the exit to get out on the parade ground and take up their posts. I managed to get backstage and do a quick change into my own uniform, got the wig off − but I forgot about the make-up!

'You've guessed it. I scrambled out with my rifle and pack and lined up with the others. I was in the back row and standing smartly to attention when this young officer marched briskly along the ranks to make sure we were good and ready for whatever Jerry might throw at us.

'He stopped abruptly opposite me, looked me up and down, but said nothing. Then he just stared into my chalk-white face, and I remembered the mascara and lipstick. Cor − strewth! I felt some explanation might be in order.

' "Er − concert party, sir . . . The alert went −"

'He just looked at me. "Um," he said. "So it did." And he moved off, only more slowly. At the end of the row he turned and peered at me, shaking his head slowly.

'The rest of the lads never let me live that one down.'

Frankie had what is known as a 'quiet war'. Instead of posting him to the front line, the Army had the sense to see that the talents of their ham-fisted but willing recruit were more suited to a microphone than to a bayonet. Gunner Howard F.A. stayed on at Shoeburyness and was transferred to the Quartermaster's Office where he virtually took over the garrison's 'fun factory'. He ousted the Entertainments Officer, and flung himself whole-heartedly into getting together the weekly acts that, for a couple of hours at least, would take the minds of the troops off what was happening across the Channel.

Along with the job, he was promoted to Bombardier. Since the only bombarding Gunner Howard had ever done in his life was the verbal kind, delivered from a stage or maybe a table-top, Frankie was a-*mazed* to be singled out.

But his enthusiasm, coupled with his need for perfection even in those young, headstrong days, tended to get the better of him and outstrip diplomacy. It would happen again and again in later life, putting people's backs up, getting himself a reputation as a niggler and worrier, both of which were fully justified. Or as a troublemaker, which wasn't.

But who could tell a general that, when a two-page memorandum landed on the top-brass desk from a stripling in the lowest ranks telling him what was wrong with the Army?

'I knew I shouldn't have done it,' Frankie would accept later. 'But as far as I was concerned too many of the officers were putting their noses in where they didn't belong. I was in charge of the shows, and there they were telling me what to do! Most of them didn't know their funny-bone from their elbow, if you get my meaning.'

So he sat down and shot off a broadside to the garrison Commander-in-Chief, outlining his grievances. Mainly it was about the blue-pencil censorship, scratching out too many of his best lines. But there was more. Frankie demanded this, he demanded that.

The apoplectic general, slamming the pages down on his blotter in disbelief, demanded his head.

The upshot: Bombardier Howard was put on a charge and thrown into the guardhouse. It ready bleakly: gross insubordination.

Frankie wriggled out of that one, but it was a close call. The C-in-C relented after apologies and a long explanation was read out to him, plus an invitation to see the next show for himself. Frankie even won recognition for an Entertainments Committee from all ranks to oversee the acts.

It was now that Frankie started to embroider his delivery with the mannerisms that would make it unique in years to come. The stumbling hesitations became more pronounced. Innocent words sprouted horns of wickedness. His leer took on new dimensions of suggestiveness.

And the boys and girls in khaki loved it.

As his confidence grew, Frankie joined a local concert party in nearby Westcliff. On his way to rehearse, he spotted a poster. Talent Night in Town! Frankie altered course, made his way to the Empire Theatre, and was first in the queue. There were no lights outside because of blackout regulations. Most of the audience were elderly. The atmosphere was curiously sombre. Frankie thought he would liven it up.

He bounced out on stage, brimful of pep. 'Good evening, ladies and gentlemen − ' Not gentle-*men*, not yet. 'I am now going to sing a little song entitled "She Sits Among the Cabbages and Peas"!' There was a stunned silence. From the wings Frankie heard an enraged hiss. The manager.

'Gerroff! Now − !'

Frankie, flummoxed, looked at the drapes and his voice rose in an indignant squeak. 'Eh? What − ?'

A ripple of laughter ran through the audience, but the manager would not be thwarted. 'I'm not having dirty jokes like that in my theatre!' he fumed. 'Out you go!' And behaving like 'Disgusted of Westcliff', he ordered the bewildered comic out of his theatre.

Much later Frankie would remember that night and work it into his act, talking to an invisible presence in the wings.

It was with the concert party, playing to local institutes in church halls, that Frankie met Mrs Vera Roper, a vivacious housewife who was a dab hand at the piano. She would accompany him when he burst into song. But one night Frankie started off . . . to silence. He stopped short, glared at her, and said: 'Are you ready?' No reply.

'That's all I need,' Frankie growled. 'A deaf accompanist!'

And that was how 'Don't mock the afflicted' came into being.

Mrs Vera Roper had, in fact, been mulling over her ration book which lay on top of the piano, counting the number of meat coupons that were left in it. She was far too preoccupied to take in Frankie's sarcasm.

He looked at her again, then at the audience. 'Poor dear,' he said scathingly. 'She's past it!'

The laughter that rose from the chairs in the hall gave him pause to think. The song got going finally, with Mrs Roper's ration book tucked safely back in her handbag. But Frankie was unusually silent in the van ride home to base.

For the next week he was engrossed in a weird and wonderful idea. On the surface it sounded too silly to work: a singer accompanied by a totally deaf pianist — how on earth could it be feasible? But slowly it took shape, and the preliminary sketch became a running gag that was probably the most famous in Frankie Howerd's entire repertoire.

During the next fifty years, Frankie would have no fewer than eight 'deaf' lady pianists tinkling the ivories. Each one benign and bewitching in her own way, each a stoic pin-cushion for her master's cruel barbs. *'No, don't laugh . . . poor soul, it might be one of your own —'* The long-suffering Vera became 'Madame Vere-Roper, known to me as Ada'. Why was it so funny? It was the way he told it, of course.

Next in line for musical immortality was Blanche Moore — 'Madame Blanchie Moore' — a large, motherly woman who stuck valiantly by him in theatres, concert halls and clubs up and down the country. She hailed from that same concert party, though at that time she only played for her two daughters while they performed a lively dance routine.

She, too, was a housewife, happy to be called on by Frankie for various dates, with the understanding that the family came first. If she was free, with no domestic commitments, she would be on the next train to whichever venue awaited her talents. If not, no problem. Frankie had other ladies-in-waiting.

Until four years later — when Sunny Rogers, the whip-cracking, rope-twirling Gal from the Golden West, rode into town.

4

On the Road

In 1942 Bombardier Howard was transferred to Wales, and found himself ensconsed in an Army Experimental Station in a remote coastal area near Swansea. It was while he was there, pushing a pen for Requisitions by day and writing comedy sketches with it by night, that word of an Army concert party called *Stars in Battledress* reached his ears. It had been formed on the lines of ENSA to boost the morale of the boys at various bases along the Allied Front. It could mean being sent into Europe or North Africa or to the Far East, wherever a war zone was located.

Frankie volunteered the same day he heard about it. In all, he volunteered four times − but on each occasion his audition was given the thumbs-down. If a bad workman blames his tools, and a bad comic is tempted to blame his material, Frankie, who was by now a remarkably good comic, must be unique in this case in being able to blame his audience. Of one.

The lone stranger was the 'interviewing officer', who behind the pips and a bored expression sat alone in large empty Nissen huts while the would-be stars in battledress did their best to impress him. Frankie needed a full house, a large audience to tease along. His '*Oooh, no − now lis-sen!*' had the hollow echo of failure, and he knew it almost before he left the hut to await the verdict a week later.

It was their loss − but in those days, who could know? Frankie tried not to feel disillusioned, but it wasn't easy. Especially for a performer whose opinion of himself seesawed wildly between adrenalin-fuelled buoyancy and the stricken depths of self-doubt. The station was too small to warrant a regular concert, so he joined a local amateur dramatic society to keep his feet near the footlights.

The war dragged on. The only significant event in Frankie's life was when he was promoted to Sergeant, and put in charge of a large Army lorry packed with soldiers. With only half a dozen driving lessons behind him − 'Well, there's the Army for you, always ready to test new talent' – Frankie lost control inside a minute, and drove the giant vehicle through a hedge and into a tree. No one was hurt, and Frankie never got behind a driving-wheel again in his life.

His brother Sidney was in the RAF and sister Betty was doing her bit for King and Country in the ATS. Frankie was actually part of the D-Day force that set out for the dawn invasion on 6 June, but neither the Germans nor more than a boat-load of men in his own Royal Artillery battalion were aware of it. The merchant ship that took him across to the beaches was unable to disembark its troops because of heavy seas, and wallowed in the swell until the first wave of the invasion had long passed on its way. Frankie was only dimly aware of what was going on – to boils and pneumonia, add sea-sickness.

He was posted to Lille, then transferred to Brussels as part of the Military Establishment. Frankie would tell a hilarious story of how he personally liberated Holland, simply by being in the first staff car to arrive at The Hague after his convoy became lost in fog. His bewildered uniformed figure was hoisted aloft by cheering crowds, and carried shoulder high through the cobbled streets. 'I was even asked for my autograph,' he said. There's a first time for everything.

Frankie was demobbed three months after VE Day brought the war to its final end. He had served six years and given of his best. And if he had made little obvious dent in the German war machine, those noisy nights in a smoke-filled Mess would prove a useful training ground for his future forays into the front line. Like other wartime entertainers, Frankie had instinctively acquired the special gift of getting through to fighting men in battlegrounds across the world. He would put it to good use.

Meanwhile he had a living to earn. And no real qualifications, apart from a one-page reference from a Major Richard Stone, who later became an agent, in appreciation of his concert party efforts.

So began the daily slog around West End agents. It was tiring, demoralizing and ultimately mind-numbing. Immediately after the war was a period when cinemas and live theatre were on the upswing, reflecting the euphoria of the times. People wanted to laugh, to be entertained. With no television to keep them glued to the flickering screen in their homes, they went out looking for their fun. Music halls were packed. Variety was king, and Frankie was desperate to be one of the courtiers.

But the agents were all powerful. Without their backing, it was almost impossible for a struggling hopeful to get on the boards — although Norman Wisdom, with admirable tenacity, had managed it. He had hounded the owner of Collins Music Hall for three weeks until the poor man finally succumbed to his pleadings and gave him a week's work — paying him a fiver, which the Scrooge immediately took back as commission.

It was a hard world and you had to have enormous faith in yourself to survive. Frankie grew used to climbing flights of wooden stairs in Soho backstreets, where he'd sit with other hopefuls on hard chairs in a small room waiting for the summons into the inner sanctum. He got to recognize the same faces, thumbing through dog-eared copies of *The Stage*, the performers' Bible. And always it was the same. 'I must have tramped across half London every week,' he said. 'They would ask: "*What are you working in now?*" Honestly! The daftness of it.

' "Nothing," I'd tell them. "If I was working I wouldn't need you, would I?" That's common sense, isn't it? But somehow it still got me nowhere.'

Nowhere, that is, until he chanced on an agent named Harry Lowe. 'Tell you what,' said Harry, taking pity on the dejected figure sitting across the desk from him. 'Why don't you get yourself a spot on the Stage Door Canteen, and I'll come to see you.' That was one option Frankie hadn't tried, mainly because the Stage Door Canteen didn't pay any money. It was an ex-Servicemen's bar in Piccadilly, with an adjoining concert hall where big names entertained the Services, waiving their fees, and the supporting acts came from the ranks. The atmosphere was one of beer mats and nostalgia, and Frankie, putting an inquiring nose round the door, felt instantly at home.

There was one snag. Civilians weren't allowed on the stage unless they were topping the bill, by invitation.

Undeterred, Frankie hurried back to his bedroom in Eltham, opened the battered suitcase he'd left on top of his wardrobe and pulled out the uniform he had folded neatly away, never really

expecting to use it again. And off went Sergeant F.A. Howard
that same afternoon, taking the bus to Piccadilly, and all the time
in a sweat in case a redcap military policeman tapped him on the
shoulder and demanded to see his papers.

He marched into the secretary's office, snapped to a smart
salute, and produced the creased reference from Major Stone. And
to his astonishment was told: 'All right. You're on next week.
Friday, seven o'clock sharp.'

Frankie raced for the phone in the corner of the bar, and called
up the agent. 'I'll be there,' Harry promised.

Butterflies once again, having a field day. But looking out at
a familiar sea of faces in uniform, Frankie felt the nerves dissipate,
to be replaced by a feeling of sudden elation. There was no sign
of Harry Lowe, but he presumed the agent was somewhere at the
back, watching from the shadows. And Frankie gave it all he'd
got, the big butcher's hands flying about as he patrolled the stage,
pressing the palms together, squeezing his nose, pulling at his chin,
regaling the audience with his Army adventures until they were
dissolved into helpless laughter. Especially D-Day. That was the
one, he recalled later, that went down best. *'There I was, rolling
about in the scuppers . . . yes, the scuppers, well and truly
scuppered I was . . . And pea-green . . . don't laugh if you haven't
tried it, sir . . . Oh, I see by your shirt that you 'ave . . . Never
mind, it'll wash out . . .'*

And the cowardly approach. As a raw sentry, he told them,
he jumped out of his skin when the sergeant crept up on him.
'What would you 'ave done if I'd really been a German?' bellowed
the sarge.

'I've already done it!' was the anguished reply.

That night was a riotous success, apart from one slight
drawback – Harry Lowe never turned up.

'I went out, flogged myself to death, and thought: "This is it,
Francis. You're in!" But when I looked for him afterwards –
no sign. I was sickened. I'd put so much into it, built up all my
hopes. What a let-down.'

Not entirely. By luck, another agent had dropped by for a drink
in the bar that night. Attracted by the gusts of laughter from the
hall, Stanley Dale walked over and slipped inside the door to stand
quietly at the back. Stanley, then with the powerful Jack Payne

agency, would later carve his own niche as the man reputed to have the biggest private collection of music hall posters in Britain. He would also become Frankie's manager. Right then, he was just starting out.

He didn't waste time or mince his words. As the downcast comic trudged towards the exit, Stanley grabbed him by the sleeve. 'Would you like us to represent you?'

Frankie gaped at him. Ex-bandleader Jack Payne was one of the most influential agents in the business and an impresario who could put on his own shows too. Forgetting all about the danger of being run in for impersonating a member of the armed forces, Frankie said yes on the spot — and went home to tell his mum. Edith Howard was thrilled for her son.

But first there was one more hurdle to overcome. Frank Barnard was the agency's general manager and vetted all the applicants wanting to be taken on the books. Florid, stocky and intimidating, Barnard put the fear of God into any newcomer who passed nervously within the portals of his office. But his reasoning was simple. If the hopeful could survive the first ten minutes with him, he could win over an audience.

Frankie had his first taste of it when he faced the formidable presence over a large glass-topped desk and a haze of cigar smoke two floors above Mayfair. A piano stood in one corner of the office. Barnard glowered at him. 'Well,' he barked. 'Have you got your band parts?'

Frankie had come with full hopes but empty pockets. No sheet music. No accompanist. He had had no idea he was on trial and supposed to give an audition.

'Er — do you have anyone who can play "Three Little Fishes?" he ventured lamely.

Barnard stunned him by launching into a tirade of invective that rocked him back in his seat. The general theme was that the Jack Payne agency was not in the business of bolstering Amateur Night Out for incompetents. Poor Frankie was told to wait outside.

He was allowed to sit and run the gamut of emotions from shivering with fear to simmering with suppressed fury . . . for four hours. What he didn't know was that Stanley Dale had given him a huge build up, and that the agency was genuinely

The show that launched him. Frankie giving his all for BBC Radio's
Variety Bandbox in 1947 – at £3.15 a time

Left: Looking through the mug-shots – with his sister Betty

Below: Christmas 1950, and carols for the boys in Korea. Frankie recording with Joan Greenwood and Eric Portman at RAF Uxbridge for the troops

Left: *The Cool Mikado* – one film that Frankie preferred to forget

Below: Frankie's first film *The Runaway Bus* (1954) saw him at the wheel of a coach trying to get out of fogbound London Airport with a villain on board – plus a load of stolen bullion. He adlibbed on screen for three minutes to save the film

Bottoms Up for the Queen! Frankie as Bottom in a special performance of *A Midsummer Night's Dream* before the Queen and Prince Philip at the Old Vic. Singing the National Anthem alongside him is actress-dancer Moira Shearer

… And meeting Her Majesty afterwards

Right: Top-level conference with scriptwriters Ray Galton (left) and Alan Simpson

Below: Teapot pose – but a thoughtful look as Francis ponders how to get his own back on those gymslip rascals in *The Great St Trinian's Train Robbery* (1966)

Left: Snuggling up in the back seat of a Rolls with Elizabeth Taylor – but Richard Burton was there too. They took Frankie out for a night on the town after seeing his 1967 hit show *Way Out in Piccadilly*

Below: With the incomparable Hattie Jacques in the 1971 Thames TV comedy special *The Laughing Stock of Television*, Frankie as Lord Nelson keeps an eye out for Lady Hamilton

Above: With Joan Sims, another regular partner: this time as his computer date in *The Howerd Confessions* (Thames TV) when Frankie has to get married to inherit a bequest from his father – who succumbed in a brothel

Right: To be, or not to be – and titter if you dare!

Celebrating a Variety Club Award with uncontrolled joy

interested. It was a serious lapse in communication.

Finally Barnard summoned him back — just when Francis had worked himself into a full head of steam, and didn't care what he said. In short, he went in and gave his potential mentor an earful.

Through the clouds of anger he was dimly aware that Barnard was now the one to rock back in his seat as Frankie stammered and stuttered, first in a-mazement, then with laughter. Pulling out a handkerchief the agent wiped his eyes and said: 'OK, you're in! That was wonderful!'

'It was?' said Frankie, totally demoralized. But he was in, and that was all that mattered.

Spring, 1946. The Jack Payne organization was going through its books, preparing to go out on the road for nine long months with a variety show that would encompass every major theatre in the country. It was to be called *For the Fun of It*, and Frankie felt the excitement mounting as he got ready to embark on his first professional engagement.

This was the moment he decided to change the spelling of his name. There were just too many Howards cluttering up the cast lists, from Trevor to Arthur to Sidney, and he felt he was getting lost in the crush. So 'Frankie Howerd — The Borderline Case' was born, and found its way on to billboards up and down the country. 'At least I'll be noticed for the misprint,' he told his agents.

Someone else would be on the tour with him. A brash unknown described by Stanley Dale in a letter to BBC producers when he was giving his new client the big sell as 'A talented young impressionist who is going to make his mark'. His name was Max Bygraves.

Frankie first set eyes on Max when they found themselves reporting to the Aeolian Hall in Mayfair for an audition to appear on a BBC variety show, prior to the start of their own tour. Both of them were keyed up. Max covered his nervousness with a veneer of 'Let's go out and slay 'em'. Frankie merely looked petrified.

Frankie went in first. He did his comedy routine in a bare room with only a table and a microphone for company. Plus a glass panel through which the auditioning producer sat watching with a critical eye. Max followed, and did his impressions to the wall. At the end he felt like climbing it.

'It was a very depressing experience for both of us,' Max recalls. 'Neither of us had a chance to put our personalities across. Frank couldn't pull faces. My impressions had to be strictly sound only. We could have got away with it, but the atmosphere was all wrong.

'Frank had gone out and bought a suit specially for the audition. He chose his usual colour — brown, which he felt was warm and relaxing for the audience. He wanted to appear as if he was chatting in a pub, or had just come in off the street for a natter.

'The sleeves on the suit were too short, but when I pointed it out all Frank said was, "I know. It's deliberate. I talk with my wrists." A lot of good that did him on radio!

'Afterwards he was in a high old state. "I was bloody awful, wasn't I?" he moaned. "I couldn't stop myself ooh-ing and aah-ing . . ." '

As for Max, he swung valiantly into impressions of Hutch and all five of the Inkspots crooning 'I Don't Want to Set the World on Fire'.

He didn't. Nor did Frankie. The impression both of them made on the producer was of the kind that says 'Don't call us . . .' and they found themselves wandering disconsolately down Bond Street together, wondering if they were in the right business.

Luckily they were both on the books of the bustling Jack Payne agency, and on the variety tour of *For the Fun of It*. Bottom of the bill, but who cared? They were in, which was what mattered, and a summer of work beckoned.

First stop: the Sheffield Empire. Frankie and Max were billed on the posters in a curious little box announcing '*They're Out!*' With them was a third act, a contortionist named Pam Denton. She was a vivacious, attractive girl who tied herself happily into sinuous knots — and captivated Frankie from the moment he set eyes on her.

He had always been fascinated with speciality acts, and the more bizarre they were, the better he liked it. Women who could do strange and exciting things with their bodies or their talent were a turn-on. When he finally was able to command his own show, he always insisted on at least one 'spesh' act in his tours around the country. Blonde Joan Rhodes, the 'world's strongest woman' was one he took to Northern Ireland with his troupe. He even discovered his most famous – and long-suffering – lady pianist Sunny Rogers when she was a rope-twirling cowgirl!

Now, in that heady summer of 1946, it actually seemed on the cards that Frankie would tie this particular knot himself. 'Frank was head over heels in love with Pam, totally enamoured,' Max Bygraves recalls. 'The three of us teamed up together, and Frank and I shared a room in boarding house digs up and down the country.' But as often as not Frankie was spending more nights with her than in the room with Max.

The star of the show was singer Donald Peers. His chirpy pianist Ernie Ponticelli made up a friendly foursome as the variety 'circus' travelled the length and breadth of Britain, spending a week at each venue. They found themselves in typical theatrical digs, a gas fire in one corner, faded curtains, occasional lumpy beds, a constant smell of floor polish – and the tempting aroma of bacon and eggs to bring them downstairs for breakfast in the morning.

Four was a good number, they found. 'The landlady was pleased to see that many of us, and somehow we could make the food last longer,' says Max. The average charge was £2.10s. a week for bed, breakfast and a late evening snack after the show, with a meter for the gas and electricity. They were earning £12 a week, sometimes a quid or two more.

The variety joke about their lodgings was to say: 'I'm staying at the George and Dragon.' Meaning? 'If a man answered the door when we knocked, we'd say: "You must be George!" ' Max still chuckles at old memories – and the old jokes that went with them.

They would talk about comedy into the small hours, the adrenalin still running long after the curtain had come down on the show. One of Frankie's long-standing idols was W.C. Fields and he regaled Max, Pam and Ernie with some of the great man's patter. Like:

Fields: 'We must think of the poor.'

Stooge: 'Which poor?'

Fields: 'Us poor.'

And Frankie's favourite, with Fields sternly telling his straight man: 'Have I not been a father and mother to you?'

'Yes.'

'A brother and sister − ?'

'Yes.'

'An uncle and aunt and two cousins . . .?'

Frankie liked that one.

The tour lasted nine months, and Frankie dubbed it 'Our Tour of the Empire'. Adding: 'The Empire Sheffield, Wigan, Huddersfield, Glasgow . . .' For Frankie, they were nine of the happiest months of his life. He was ambitious, he was out on the road where he belonged, buzzing with new ideas and routines. He was among friends. And eventually he was in love − with Pam.

He wasn't bad looking, exhibiting the gauche charm of a young Michael Crawford. His insecurity, which he never bothered to hide, meant that women were drawn to him by quite simply wanting to mother him. With no financial responsibilities, Frankie was as carefree as any doubting comic can ever be when he is crippled by nightly nerves.

'Max and I were total opposites,' he would say later. 'I was in a continual state of panic. He brimmed over with confidence. I was a-mazed how we hit it off!'

But they did. Frankie would stand in the wings and observe the other two-thirds of the *They're Out!* trio. The pair of comiçs had eight minutes each, Pam had six. Max would return the compliment, and afterwards all three would hold an inquest over supper, comparing notes. Frankie was living dangerously, an unknown comic daring to face his audience full-frontal, so to speak, and talk to them, berate them − '*What, are you deaf or something?*' − and generally look like a man who was in the wrong place at the wrong time. After his monologue, he finished his act with 'Three Little Fishes', the song where listeners had been known to break their chairs in helpless laughter − or to sit po-faced until the final sardine (as he privately referred to them) swam out of sight over that famous dam.

'Frank would go out and bait his audience,' Max recalls. 'He was living on a knife-edge on that stage. Don't forget we were all unknown. He'd insult them, pretend to forget his lines − then miraculously remember them just before it got embarrassing. When it worked it was great. I've seen him tear the place up, and it was wonderful to watch. Other times . . .'

In those days the 'communication problem' across the north–south divide was acute. Max was safe with his impressions, Frankie often fared less well. Ernie Wise, who later became a good friend, was more aware of it than most. 'It was like the Berlin Wall,' he says. 'That was why Eric and I took such a long time to be discovered!'

From Sheffield they went to Nottingham, then on the circuit to Liverpool, Manchester, Newcastle, Sunderland and all stations north to Glasgow, where the Empire Theatre, notorious 'graveyard of the comics', awaited them like some Dracula's Castle, the inmates anxious to draw blood.

An incident in Sunderland did little to help Frankie's peace of mind. Max remembers it well. 'It was the first time we really saw the dividing line across the country. Everyone had talked about it, of course. But in some places they just didn't get Frankie at all. I'm not sure they could understand what he was even saying, let alone his humour.

'One night Frank was in the middle of his act when there was an almighty crack from the stage, like a whip. It completely threw him. He dried up, then got going again – but he couldn't wait to get off. No one knew what it was. But after the curtain came down at the end we all had a search around, and a stagehand found a ship's rivet that someone up in the gods had thrown! It was brand new.

'A lot of shipyard workers used to come to the shows. But if it had hit him it could have killed him.'

In the dressing-room afterwards Frankie was still shaking. He pulled himself together enough to say: 'Obviously they can't afford tomatoes up 'ere!'

'But after that he was a nervous wreck for the rest of the Sunderland run, and couldn't wait to shake the dust of the place off his heels. He was terrified of an audience like that.' Max still remembers Frankie's anguish.

They reached Glasgow on a blustery autumn day, and took an apprehensive look at the mausoleum-like theatre in Sauchiehall Street that would be their abode for the next six nights. Two houses, 6.15 p.m. and 8.30 p.m. Frankie had an immediate attack of the colly-wobbles and headed for the nearest loo backstage. He had a feeling he would get to know it quite well.

The Empire's reputation as a comics' graveyard actually referred to Cockney comics, but also to any Sassenach who dared venture across the border from down south. The audience could be as generous with their praise as they were with their retribution. One manager who lasted seven long years there is Stan Jarvis, now in charge of the Globe Theatre in the West End, who – as Frankie once put it – has dined out on more stories about the Empire than he'd had hot dinners.

'It was no myth,' Stan assures his listeners. 'Most English comics died there. Everything you ever heard about the place was justified, and the customers took pride in their reputation. It was a brave man who faced them. We didn't say: "Will we get trouble tonight?" We said: "Where will it be?" '

Mr Jarvis would later reminisce with Frankie about his own baptism of fire as a greenhorn young assistant, left in charge in his first week when the manager went home early. 'A group of three hundred employees from a local bakery firm came in to celebrate. Half-way through the second half the "screwtaps" started flying on to the stage – screw tops from the beer bottles. One hit the conductor on the head. He was bald and unfortunately it drew blood. The music came to a grinding halt and he evacuated the orchestra pit. It looked like a full scale riot was about to happen, so I rang down the curtain. It took the police half an hour to clear the theatre. I wouldn't have wanted to tell that story to Frankie at the time.'

Into such myth and legend the hapless Francis rode. Out on to the stage he stepped, feeling an ominous rumbling in his stomach and wondering if he should have been wearing bicycle clips. But – wonder of wonders! Not only did the 'auld enemy' understand him – or if they didn't, they still found him a hoot. Every night was the same, noisy but friendly. Even Saturday, traditionally 'screwtap night'.

At the end of the week Frankie packed his bag with a mixture of euphoria and regret, and headed back to the comparative calm of the seaside piers along the south coast.

Some years later, at one of the peaks of his career, Frankie went back to the Glasgow Empire with his own show. He wowed the Scots every night – until the final Saturday. One of the numbers called for Frankie to clamber on to the knee of his feed, Lee

Young, who was several stone lighter, and sing 'Climb up on my Knee, Sunny Boy!' as if he were a ventriloquist's dummy. But as his soulful tones rang out, boos erupted from all parts of the theatre. Shouts of: 'Will ye get off the wee man!' echoed through the auditorium.

Lew Lane, who was watching from the wings, remembers the effect it had. 'Frankie looked absolutely stunned. He couldn't understand what he had done wrong. All week they'd loved him. But it seems the audience felt little Lee was being put upon in some way — I know it sounds ridiculous, but that's what we heard afterwards. The show never recovered and everyone was glad when the curtain rang down that night without further trouble.' Score one more headstone for the Glasgow Empire.

The sad epilogue for the famous theatre came when the Cockney Comics' Graveyard in turn was buried by the developers in the dubious name of progress. In 1963 it was pulled down to make way for an office block. Frankie felt there should be a roll of honour for all comics who had played there — and survived. With his own name high on the list.

The sad epilogue to the tour for Frankie was that at the end of it Pam Denton left him. Frankie told his closest friends that they had become 'unofficially engaged'. Pam obviously thought otherwise. She eventually married an American acrobatic dancer and was last heard of living in the US. 'Frankie was pretty devastated,' says Max, sad for his old pal. 'He adored her.'

5
Radio Waves

The Tour of the Empire was over. Back home in Eltham with his mum, Frankie hardly had time to draw breath before a messge came through. Stanley Dale, telling him to get along to the Aeolian Hall, double-quick, to audition for *Variety Bandbox*. Frankie could hardly believe his ears.

The hour-long Sunday night *Bandbox* was the show everyone, but *everyone* wanted to be on. With cinemas closed on Sundays, and TV not even a gleam in the corner of the room, the country tuned in to the radio – and this was the one they listened to. Even the biggest stars needed no persuasion at all from the producer, an energetic lady named Joy Russell-Smith, to spend their Sundays locked away in rehearsal before the red light went on at 6.00 p.m. and they were on the air.

Frankie reported back to the same studio where, just a few months before, he and Max Bygraves had been given the proverbial bum's rush. This time he found the walls had been piled up with sandbags, presumably to deaden any echo as well as sound-proof the room. He had to stand with his back to the glass panel, so that all the producer and her assistant could see was the back of his reddening neck – pink, because Frankie felt more flummoxed than ever. An audience of sandbags! He stuttered and stammered through his script as if he was a four-year-old learning to read, and was convinced he had come another cropper.

Instead, Joy came out beaming. 'Wonderful,' she exclaimed. 'It's so – different.' That it was, for sure. No one had ever heard anything like Frankie at his most nervous trying to put his patter across, voice only. On 12 October 1946 Joy wrote to Stanley Dale in Jack Payne's office, calling him by his nickname of 'Scruffy', and saying simply: '*Frankie – very funny, original patter. Seeded.*' It sounds like Wimbledon, but it meant he was given another test, this time in front of a guinea-pig audience of fellow actors. He passed with flying colours, and was paid four handsome guineas for his trouble.

At that time the whizz-kid making most waves in radio was a slim, dapper young man with a penchant for herringbone waistcoats, named Dennis Main Wilson. An ex-Cavalry officer with bright blue eyes that radiated humour and mischief behind huge spectacles, Dennis was only twenty-three when he came out of the Army and into Light Entertainment to oversee the new wave from the Forces. He would swiftly become one of the legendary names in the BBC.

Even in those days the 'old school' in the Corporation were calling this upstart in their midst 'over-eager and self-opinionated'. Ignoring the disapproving grunts from on high, Dennis started sweeping the tide of ex-service comedy talent with a wide net. Minnows who would become whales included Tony Hancock, Max Bygraves, Alfred Marks, Harry Secombe, Spike Milligan, Eric Sykes – and Frankie Howerd.

Dennis found they had something in common: as a kid he had been living in the next street to Arbroath Road, just a few yards from Frankie's own home. Now he was senior producer in charge of auditioning the ranks, sifting out talent – 'Like Leading Aircraftman Monkhouse R., who confessed many years later he had been using Jack Benny material,' says Dennis. 'It didn't matter. He was too bright to lose.

'Frankie was lucky to have Joy as his producer. She was a brilliant woman, an enormous enthusiast. And she couldn't resist Frankie's humour. She put him into the show as resident comedian on alternate weeks with Derek Roy. It ran for ages, and they adopted the American style of insulting each other all the time. It worked beautifully.'

Frankie's famous opening line 'Now, ladies and gentle-*men*!' was first heard at 6.00 p.m. on Sunday, 1 December 1946, a date that would mean more than any other at that phase in his career. Immediately it became his calling card. He was paid £18 for the early shows, and would remain in residence for a run of two and a half hit years. Top of the ratings – the audience figures hit an incredible fifteen million. Top of the tree. Frankie's verbal twitching became his trademark. Soon he was adding other phrases like 'Just make meself comfy', which in other hands would probably have met with only stony silence, but coming from this shambling bundle of nerves reduced the studio to hysterics.

On that first bill, which came live from the Palace Theatre, Camberwell, were Jessie Matthews, Stéphane Grappelli, and Johnny Riscoe, with the programme introduced by Brian Reece, later to plod the beat as 'PC 49'.

Frankie was more aware than anyone that a comic is only as good as his material. Unlike a variety tour where he could use the same sketches every week in a different town, radio simply ate up the ideas. And in those days the performer paid his scribes out of his salary — if Frankie was getting £25 for a show, £10 would go to the scriptwriter.

It was at this time, with *Bandbox* going strong, that a letter came out of the blue that would play a key role in Frankie's fortunes. It was forwarded on to Sheffield, where he was playing Simple Simon (who else?) in the Christmas pantomime *Jack and the Beanstalk*. The writer felt he could be of some use when it came to scripts. He signed himself Eric Sykes.

Frankie invited him up to Sheffield for a chat. In his dressing-room it was apparent that this could be just the creative mind he was looking for. Frankie discussed his own approach to humour, and listened intently to Eric's own ideas. 'Most people understand jokes about mothers-in-law, kitchens, sex and lavatories,' Eric reasoned. 'I don't think jokes about politicians, for instance, make people laugh as much as basic everyday difficulties.' He also believed in the old saying: 'A comedian is not someone who says funny things, but someone who says things funnily.'

Sykes would take those everyday difficulties and transport them into the realms of hysterical fantasy. Some of the gems he invented have gone down in the annals of broadcasting. He knew that with radio he could tune in to the imagination of the listening millions and unravel any situation from the sublime into the totally ridiculous. How else could Frankie be stuck on Crewe station with a couple of elephants, only to have one escape into a cinema and sit there blocking the view of the row behind until it was dragged out? Another classic was Frankie learning to be a lion-tamer — '*What, me go in there? I told them straight: Not on your nellie!*'

Eric had been earning £3 a week in repertory doing his own stand-up comedy act. Frankie had the same ability to see the silly side of life, and they found their personalities were similar. Eric would write for Frankie for the next ten years, a decade that would be one of the most fruitful of his career.

Sykes says now: 'You can only write for people you really understand. You have to get to know the man as a friend, it can never be just a business arrangement. Then you start to study them technically, by watching them perform until you know exactly what they can do and what they can't.

'It's the little things you have to pick up — whether they get a laugh best with a line or with just a look. Frankie always added something to any script. He was never a straight actor playing a part.'

Eric has fought a long and courageous battle with deafness and Frankie, working closely with him for so many years, believed he could trace it back to an evening at the Blackpool Swimming Baths in 1949. He watched Eric plummet in an impressive swallow dive from the top board — but his entry into the water made an inglorious splash. Frankie, seeing his friend shake his head and try to clear it, was convinced the trouble started from that moment.

Back at the *Bandbox*, the faked feud with Derek Roy, inspired by the long-standing American air-waves vendetta between Jack Benny and Fred Allen, helped the fun along. Frankie would take the mickey relentlessly out of Derek's own signature tune, 'I'm Doctor Roy the Melody Boy', and Derek cheerfully responded in kind.

Dennis Main Wilson started his own show from the Garrick Theatre — ironically, the scene of Frankie's last West End triumph before his death — and brought his new find over to join the gang. This was a spectacular by any standard, particularly for a radio show, complete with a 24-piece orchestra and major stars booked from all over the world. 'I got Frankie in as resident, brought in Derek Roy, and kept the feud going to fuel the listening figures. The audience loved it.

'On the very last programme, we brought them together. And there was Derek Roy sitting on Frankie's knee with the pair of them singing the old Eddie Cantor number "When there are grey skies . . . I don't mind those grey skies — 'cos you make them blue — *Sunny Boy*!" It brought the house down. It was one of the greatest spoof knockabouts for two comedians we ever put on.'

Frankie had yet to try that one on the Glasgow Empire. Bert Weedon, the veteran guitarist, recalls that even then Francis was giving his all to 'Three Little Fishes' − subtitled, for the connoisseur of such melodies 'Itty Bitty Poo'. Along with 'Autumn Leaves' it became Frankie's best-known song, a unique rendering which has taken its place in the annals of popular music. Particularly with the tone deaf.

> 'Down in the meadow in a little bitty pool
> Swam three little fishes and a mama fishy too −
> "Swim", said the mama fishy, "swim if you can",
> And they swam and they swam all over the dam . . .'

It was when Francis got into overdrive that the place fell apart. His voice, oscillating on all decibel levels, would shriek: '*Boop-boop dit-tem dot-tem what-tem Chu!*' and repeat it until it actually seemed to make sense. Quite what a certain Saxie Dowell, who wrote it back in 1939, would have made of this spluttering exposition is not on record. Others have tried, from Ben Lyon and Bebe Daniels to Pinky and Perky and Glenn Miller. But Frankie left his own indelible stamp on that song and fins would never be the same again.

Bert Weedon, who as part of that 24-piece orchestra was backing Frankie's vocal efforts, remembers it well. 'His voice? Let me think. I'd call it − mediocre,' he said, picking the word carefully.

Variety Bandbox was the springboard for Frankie's career. The chance he had been waiting for throughout the long, frustrating days and nights of an apprenticeship he thought would never end.

He signed a new contract with the Jack Payne organization, one that sadly in six years' time would end in tears and recriminations in the High Court. But for now Frankie was off and running, fêted alike by the BBC and his growing army of fans.

He was still plagued by doubts, and always would be. Now he took to lonely walks in the country, or finding a convenient cemetery where he would rehearse his lines to rows of impassive headstones. Not a single titter there − but Frankie found it curiously creative, and calming too.

*

Those radio days were wine and roses to the rising star. Frankie was able to take off to Clacton for the lucrative 1947 summer season, catching the early train for a Sunday trip back to London for all-day rehearsals and the live 6.00 p.m. *Bandbox*. The following year he starred in a revue at the Shepherd's Bush Empire for a young impresario named Bernard Delfont, who was just cutting his teeth in the world of variety. It was called *Ta-Ra-Ra-Boom-De-Ay*, and on the strength of his radio popularity, Frankie topped the bill. It was to be the start of a long and fruitful association.

'I remember standing at the back of the theatre every night,' recalls Bernie (now Lord) Delfont. 'The place was jammed, packed solid. Even Frankie was astonished at his own popularity.'

Frankie was still not sure what had hit him, how he had leaped from lowly comic to top-of-the-bill in virtually one mighty bound. He tried to reason it thus: 'Radio fame in those days was like TV or pop success later. Also the public were curious to know what I looked like. All they'd had to go on was my voice, and they wanted to see the ugly mug that went with it.' Francis, modest as ever. 'I was a-mazed when it turned out that I was one of the biggest draws in the country.'

If proof were needed, he worked every week of that rich harvest year, touring the country with *Ta-Ra*, dashing back to London on Sundays for *Bandbox*, and ending up in spectacular style with the sell-out pantomime *Jack and the Beanstalk* at the Prince of Wales for a Christmas bonus.

Meanwhile, within the corridors of power at the BBC, Frankie Howerd was making his own air-waves. The top brass knew they had a rare talent on their hands, one to nurture and sustain. They also had an artistic tiger by the tail. Even faced with professionals with years of broadcasting experience behind them, Frankie fretted and fumed, found fault with the tiniest irritant, and on a bad day could be impossible.

His attention to detail was microscopic. His reasoning? Simple. He had taken endless trouble to get it perfect, so everyone else must hold the same high ground. How much trouble? Like rehearsing his lines up to seventy times to get it right, *even when he only had to read them*. There's devotion to duty for you — but it was Frankie's way.

Useless to plead they were doing their best, that it wasn't their fault a fuse had blown or the wrong 'Gelly' (filter) had been put in the spotlight. Frankie fiddled and fussed, he was rude to technicians, he drove everyone into a state of exasperation, bordering on near-hysteria, often minutes before the show went out.

But they put up with him, because when you've got a budding genius standing six feet away who also happens to be the most popular comic in broadcasting, you learn to live with it.

The squalls were short, sharp and swiftly over. Once the red light glowed, the spotlight embraced him, and Frankie was at the mike, the only histrionics were the ones in the script. And with another successful show over, and the audience smiling and chattering their way out into Camden Town (in the early days, later into Lower Regent Street), all was sweetness and light. Frankie would go round saying sorry to anyone he'd insulted, and frequently take the entire production crew and some of the cast out to dinner. Up to a dozen would sit down at a hastily reserved table overlooking the Thames at the Elephant on the River, one of the most expensive restaurant-clubs in London, and order whatever they liked. Frankie paid. 'He was exceedingly generous,' said one recipient of his host's largesse. 'But we never knew until the actual night whether we'd be going off for a five-course feast – or heading home for a cheese sandwich.'

Frankie was not the sort to bear grudges – indeed, he would worry for days on end that he might have hurt someone's feelings. 'Did I go too far? Are you sure he's not upset?' he would ask his manager Dennis Heymer, needing reassurance. Dennis would pat his arm soothingly. 'It'll be fine, Frank. Don't worry.'

The first cloud on the horizon of euphoria appeared on 23 February 1948, with a chilly memo from Tom Chalmers, Acting Controller of the Light Programme, to the Head of General Overseas Programmes. It asked crisply: 'Did you hear *Variety Bandbox* on Sunday? Frankie Howerd was obviously screamingly funny to the audience with a lot of "business" which did not mean a thing to the listeners. It meant so much to him however that his stooge dried up at one point, while he himself got completely lost in his script soon after. You will no doubt want to take this up with the Head of Variety.' Oh dear. Black mark, and officially logged, too, as all inter-office memos are at the BBC.

But was he worth all the hassle? By May 1948 Frankie's fee with *Variety Bandbox* had gone up to £26.5s. (£26.25), which would hardly break the bank, but was the going rate. That sum even included the services of the accompanist, but there was a further £5.5s. (£5.25) reproduction fee for the World Service as a bonus. Any repeat fees were agreed at £13.2s.6d. (£13.12).

Despite misgivings in certain high places, Frankie's *Bandbox* contract, along with that of Derek Roy, was extended until the last week of 1948. And finally the powers-that-be relented, and acknowledged the seam of gold they had stumbled upon.

In July 1949 Michael Standing, the Head of Variety himself (known as HV), was penning a note to his chiefs: 'Unquestionably, as a result of his broadcasts on *Variety Bandbox*, Frankie Howerd has become a star of the first magnitude. He is now among the first four drawing names in the country. The latter fact alone would appear to entitle him to a substantial radio fee.' (Auntie was about to unbutton her purse.) 'This is further supported by the undeniable truth that he is a very fine comedian. We shall certainly not be able to get him for a fee of less than sixty guineas (£66).' Quite what that would do to the licence fee remained unclear. What was self-evident was that Frankie was value for money. A lot of money.

Thirteenth of October was another big day in Frankie's 1949 calendar. He returned to *Variety Bandbox*, and yet again people were switching on for their favourite Sunday night comic opiate. By May 1950 Frankie had earned himself the title of 'Most popular BBC comedian'.

But after all those months on *Bandbox*, Frankie was growing restless. His career had become one long curtain call of cheers and applause, but he wanted to spread his wings still wider. The ambition that would eventually drive him into a nervous breakdown was beginning to create the first ominous cracks in the shell.

He started to rattle the chains that bound him to his weekly variety spot. In a personal letter to Standing, dated 31 July 1950, Frankie put it on the line. 'I would like to go forward, while retaining my present popularity. By going forward, I mean to embark upon something a little more ambitious and a little different from the "patter act" on which I have hitherto mainly relied . . .'

Three days later he got a terse reply. 'I respect your views about your radio future, but I am afraid that I do not entirely share them,' wrote HV. In short the message was: 'Get back to the *Bandbox*.'

Frankie mulled this rebuff over for ten days, before sending off the letter that severed him once and for all from the show that had made him a household name throughout the country. 'I regret from a purely personal point of view . . . that I cannot contemplate a return to *Variety Bandbox*. I feel I must on principle dig my heels in over the matter.'

Was he digging himself an early radio grave? Standing sent a brief memo to his senior men: 'Howerd does not want to do *Bandbox*, so we must leave it at that.'

By 1951 Frankie had his own show, a mixture of sit-coms and stand-up monologues where he would take the audience on, and have the place falling apart with laughter almost before the theatre flies were open.

'I shall begin this eisteddfod tonight with a promise that you shall not go home titterless. Titterless ye shall not go . . . quiet please, a modicum of shush, now . . . Right . . . There was a young salesman from Leeds, who swallowed a packet of seeds. He got covered in grass . . . wait for it, WAIT for it . . . You may be wrong, you know . . . From his nose to his toes . . . And he had to sit down in his weeds . . . aaah, you see, you WERE wrong . . . There's no filth 'ere, y'know. How dare you titter at my ditty . . .'

Frankie Howerd walked his tightrope between good taste and bad with consummate ease, but elsewhere people were having kittens. The BBC was ultra-sensitive about offending its vast audience, understandably so. Frankie's fixation with the private areas of the human anatomy was dangerous ground.

A stern rebuke from on high for the Assistant Director of Variety in 1948 spelled it out. 'I am afraid you have slipped up rather badly in allowing Harry Secombe to refer to paranoiac schizophrenia. There is a directive to the effect that no distressing ailments must be mentioned, and as you know a considerable number of ex-servicemen are suffering from this complaint.'

The recipient of this brief but telling broadside could only reply with due humility: 'My sincere apologies. I had no idea there was such a disease. In other words I thought this thing was a gag. You can be sure in future I shall check up on the name of any disease mentioned in a script.'

Since most of Frankie's act had to do with distressing ailments of one sort of another, one can only imagine the sleepless nights endured by those in authority.

The mixed feelings Frankie roused within the portals of Broadcasting House bubbled close to the surface. On 12 January 1951, C.J. 'Con' Mahoney, the ebullient Head of Light Entertainment, dropped an official note to Tom Reynolds, one of his senior producers: 'I am simply placing on record that *The Frankie Howerd Show* is "all yours" from Sunday, 28 January.'

The note went back to him with a hand-written reply scrawled on it: 'And I would like to place on record that Frankie Howerd is *the* most difficult artist I have ever had to cope with.' Tom's experience had included ten years with the long-running *Life with the Lyons* show, by repute no easy act to control. Tom approached Frankie with the proverbial whip and chair, and came through relatively unscathed.

In the early fifties Frankie could do no wrong. He starred in the Royal Variety Shows. Another hit radio series was *Happy Go Lucky*. As Professor Howerd, Frankie welcomed a celebrity each week to his 'consulting rooms' for a 'profound discussion', and the queue grew more impressive by the minute. Names like Richard Attenborough, Claire Bloom, Donald Wolfit, Margaret Lockwood, Dirk Bogarde and Tony Hancock jostled for airtime, usually to plug the film or play they were in.

Richard Burton was at a peak in his own career, hailed as one of the great Hamlets. So it was natural that Prof Howerd would invite him to declaim the 'To be or not to be' soliloquy – and bring back a few memories to Frankie of how he didn't do it quite as well at his RADA audition.

Instead, Burton insisted on playing the trumpet.

The scripts for the show were written by a pair of unknown

young writers named Ray Galton and Alan Simpson, working
from a tiny room above a greengrocer's shop in Shepherd's Bush.
'We thought it would be rather nice if Frankie wanted to act a
big scene with Burton, but Richard wanted to blow his own
trumpet, so to speak,' Simpson recalls.

'We wrote a whole page of a classical speech for Frankie that
included every cliché in the book, from "My eyes are failing"
to "Is this the end?" Of course he wanted the great Hamlet to
perform with him, but Burton just went on tooting his trumpet.
Frankie got more and more outraged and desperate as only he
could, and it worked a treat. It was really very funny.'

Every week the star guest would do exactly the opposite of what
the Professor demanded, with hilarious results. Claire Bloom —
Frankie called her 'Clara', which did nothing for the lady's
composure — insisted on tap-dancing. Others did anything from
mime to animal impressions.

In its way, it was a radio forerunner to the style of show
perfected by Eric Morecambe and Ernie Wise at the height of their
TV success, with household names called on to do all kinds of
absurd and unlikely things.

Whatever the star's temperament, they could not ignore him.
All the BBC heads were in agreement on one indisputable fact:
Frankie Howerd was their top comedian. The orders went out
to do everything to placate his moods and keep the boy happy.
The big question was how best to use him, when, and how often.
Frankie was a willing carthorse, and if the word 'workaholic' had
been in vogue, he would have been an instant qualifier.

He drove himself mercilessly. With no personal responsibilities
or attachments, Frankie was in love with his career.

Now the BBC shifted its outside broadcasts from the Garrick
in Camden Town, and set up home in the Playhouse in the shadow
of Hungerford Bridge. Henceforth this rather gloomy old place
would become the hub of audience-participation shows, a move
that greatly displeased Frankie and caused a further *frisson* of
unease within Corporation ranks when they realized it. Frankie
was going through producers like a bowling ball in a skittle alley
and he complained bitterly about the new venue for the 1954
Frankie Howerd Show.

As his reluctant new producer Alastair Scott-Johnston

mentioned to the Assistant Head of Variety in 1954: 'I am personally not at all happy about doing the show from the Playhouse. The general acoustic qualities are inferior to Camden. Further, as you are aware, Frankie Howerd is a somewhat temperamental artist, and he has a personal antipathy towards the Playhouse. I feel sure we shall run into trouble on this score.'

The BBC succumbed. The show was shifted to the Royal Artillery Theatre in Woolwich, close to Frankie's old Army barracks. It was now that he came on a collision course with the lovely Yolande Donlan, an American comedy actress married to the man who in that same year directed Frankie's screen debut *The Runaway Bus*, Val Guest. Yolande's blonde curls and saucer eyes made her a natural for the British stage version of *Born Yesterday*. But this was one blonde who was anything but dumb when it came to having her name in lights. When she was offered a spot on the programme she insisted on it being billed as *The Frankie Howerd – Yolande Donlan Show*. Fat chance! Alastair talked it over with Frankie, and duly reported: 'Quite rightly, in my opinion, Frankie does not feel this is justified.' Yolande was out. Into her shoes stepped another lively lady in the shape of Shani Wallis.

Frankie was blissfully unaware of the correspondence going on inside 'BH' (Broadcasting House – the BBC love initials). He had no real idea of the furore that followed in his footsteps, or the inter-departmental memos humming through the in-trays and out again. He was on a high roll, and it looked as if nothing could stop him. By 1957 his shows were going out on the British Forces Network to servicemen and women across the world, and Frankie had become a Forces favourite. He followed it up personally. The RAF base at Brize Norton became a regular Departure Lounge for him as he flew off to some remote spot on the globe where a British Presence was being kept. Even if he did hate flying, and kept his eyes shut for much of the flight. Also, unknown to the general public and without any publicity banners waving, he did the rounds of the British home bases, too.

Dennis Main Wilson tells a story of how the pair of them flew out to Hamburg as the advance guard for Frankie's show in front of 2,000 soldiers and their wives in the huge Musik Halle. They checked the equipment, talked to the engineers, made sure the acoustics in the hall were right. The rest of the troupe, as well as a twelve-piece band, was due in the following day, the eve of the concert, bringing with them the music — and the script.

'By midnight there was no sign of anyone and we started to worry. Then we heard the news: thick fog in Britain. No one was flying. Next morning the fog was still there, but the team wasn't.'

Frankie was sweating more than ever. Dennis asked him: 'What do you want to do?'

'What *can* I do?' responded Frankie. 'I can't let them down.'

And without any script, he stepped out on to a large, lonely and empty stage and kept the troops in stitches for two hours, adlibbing his way through all the material he could remember.

'It was quite incredible,' says Dennis, recalling it. 'But Frankie had something in common with Bob Hope — apart from the fact that they both grew up in Eltham. He had a computer brain lodged in his subconscious. When he was going strong it linked up, and he could have gone on all bloody night! But then the team finally turned up — and he gave the full show as if those two hours had just been a warm up!'

Radio was the name of the game, and Frankie played it for all it was worth. How could he know the whistle was about to blow, that TV would take over, closing the music halls and making the public tune in to new channels of entertainment that would leave him out in the cold?

6

Sunny Interlude

If anyone was the real Missus in Frankie Howerd's life, it was Sunny Rogers. Small — just five feet, one inch — sparkling, with a smile that started up near her cheekbones and could light up an entire theatre, Sunny was Frankie's feed, friend, pianist, stooge and patient victim of his insults for thirty-five unforgettable years. The insults always fell on deaf ears — *'Poor old thing. She's past it, you know — that is, if she ever 'ad it! She's deaf — aren't you, dear? Deaf! I said deaf!'*

And Sunny would play away, fingers rippling over the keyboard to produce 'Autumn Leaves', the dazzling smile never faltering . . .

Today, in her seventies, Sunny lives in the ground floor of a red-brick two-storey terraced house in Brighton, five minutes from the sea, with her close friend Alwyn Miller, an actress turned physiotherapist, upstairs. The house looks out on to a view of Queen's Gardens, a quiet residential park that at weekends comes alive with children and courting couples.

Sunny lives alone with her memories. A picture of herself with Frankie drawn in charcoal by a local artist, Patricia Butt, hanging in the hallway by the stairs, is a constant reminder of the man who became a trusted friend and confidante for more than three decades. Some have gone so far as to say theirs was a surrogate marriage: that Sunny knew her Frankie as well as any wife ever could.

She laughs that one away — but agrees that outside his family she knew him longer than anyone, and better than most. And on stage and in the wings Sunny Rogers was most certainly Frankie's 'other half'.

The quiet garden at the back of the house is her favourite spot, a patio with three stepped layers of crazy paving, the flowerbeds neatly trimmed — gardening is her hobby — and alive with colour: bluebell-like freesia, pale pink peace roses, green shrubs and red fuchsia. A restful spot where she thinks often of Frankie and remembers the laughter that is her lasting memory of him.

Sunny is a Lancashire lass, the daughter of a grocer, born in Ashton-under-Lyme, six miles from Manchester, and has all the directness of that no-nonsense county. Her real name was Jessie, but her nickname of Smiley (long before John Le Carré thought of it) soon became Sunny — and it stuck.

Early on it was obvious that her talents lay in directions other than the academic. She was just three when her headmistress at Wellbeck Street Primary wrote to her mother: 'You really should send your little girl to dancing school. All she does is sing and dance and entertain us all day long . . .'

Naturally the little girl made her mark in the school plays, took up piano lessons at eight, and became adept at dancing and drama. 'Music, dancing, elocution, that's all that mattered,' Sunny says. And her voice lost all traces of 'Eee bah goom!' before she was in her teens.

At the tender age of fourteen, Sunny danced an audition for the Tiller Girls, and to her delight was taken under the wing of the famous dance troupe. Now, sitting in a white-cushioned chair under a parasol in her garden, in the quiet of a Sunday afternoon, sipping tea from a delicate cup of bone china, her eyes still sparkle behind her glasses as she recalls those headstrong teenage days. How she was the rebel in the family, and set her heart on show business from the day she performed her first twirl in front of the other tots in her class.

'I wasn't too happy at home. Nothing was wrong — my parents were marvellous. But I wanted to spread my wings. I just had to get away.' They put her into sequins and high heels, and made her up to look sixteen. For her first appearance on a public stage Sunny found herself at the late-night Trocadero show in a Cochran Revue, linking arms with another high-kicker, Marjorie Robertson, who would later become Anna Neagle.

Sunny became Captain of the Tiller Girls — 'I was eighteen, and ambitious' — until she was spotted by the unlikely combination of a cowboy duo named Buck and Chick, an energetic American pair from the Ol' West who pranced around the stage with a rope-twirling, gun-slinging act. They invited her to team up with them to tour Europe.

Professionally, she was still Jessie. She spent hours under Buck's tuition learning to twirl a lariat, crack a whip and become the fastest gun in the West End. It was then that Jack Payne, the agent who would later represent Frankie Howerd (with dire results to them both), spotted her, assigned his general manager Frank Barnard to look after her, and advised her to change her name to Sunny Rogers. And make it official. 'I was a happy person, and everyone talked about my marvellous smile! So I thought: why not? It fits. From then on I became Sunny.'

She first heard of Frankie Howerd when she was sitting in her agent's Mayfair office. Barnard came in with a huge smile stitched all over his normally sombre features. He beamed at her with unusual good humour and she saw his eyes were moist. 'I have just auditioned the funniest man I have ever, ever seen,' Barnard announced without preamble. 'He stood in my office with no music, nothing, and just went through what he did — and I can't stop laughing.' He wiped his eyes to prove that even strong men weep. And added: 'I hired him on the spot. His name's Frank Howard.'

That was 1946, the same year Frankie changed the spelling of his surname and became Frankie Howerd, the Borderline Case . . .

Sunny would next appear with her rope-twirling pardners at the music hall mecca for all variety artists — the Metropole in the Edgware Road. Sure enough, that week on the programme, buried away at the bottom of the line-up, was a brief billing: *They're Out*! And below it: Max Bygraves, Pamela Denton, and Frankie Howerd — the Borderline Case.

'I became very friendly with these two boys. They were in dressing-room No. 11, I was in No. 3. We just hit it off, and I'd always be in there before a show, laughing and joking with them.

'We used to try to calm Frankie's nerves — I'd never seen someone get so het up before a performance. But he was always like that. And let's face it, if you don't feel those butterflies before going out to face an audience there must be something wrong with you. But Frankie suffered more than most. The poor dear was nearly climbing the wall sometimes, he was so worked up . . .'

Frankie proposed to Sunny in Clacton-on-Sea. Not marriage

– though that was virtually how it turned out – but a professional partnership.

'The show was touring the country, and we'd reached Clacton. Frankie popped into my dressing-room, sat down, twiddled his thumbs nervously for a few moments, then said: "Sunny, would you like to do some sketches with me?"

'I said: "I'd be absolutely delighted!" And that's how the whole thing started.'

In those post-war, pre-television days, theatres were bulging – and none more so that the music halls. The Borderline Case and his fellow artistes were on the road, and in the fast lane. Sunny was now a solo act, billed as 'Sunny Rogers, the Gal from the Golden West'. And the nightly gunshots and whip-cracks echoed down esplanades the length of the country, from Blackpool to Brighton, Scarborough and Southampton, and points in between wherever there was a variety hall or a pier beckoning.

Frankie's busy pen had produced scores of sketches and he was able to try them out for size on the first house then alter it or throw it away if it didn't work in time for the second. Sunny proved a natural foil, and her sharpness and timing gave the sketches just the edge Frankie wanted. He was a perfectionist even then, and now the stuttering had come into its own, and the 'ooohs' and 'aaahs' were flowing thick and fast.

For the next twelve years Sunny would help out. Sometimes for a season, more often for a week here or there. She kept her Western costumes in her dressing-room for her own act, and would change for the comedy routines. But so far, no piano. Only sketches.

Her favourite was also one of Frankie's. The sole props were a park bench and a lollipop. Francis prances out dressed as a small boy, sucking his lollipop. He puts it down on the bench and wanders off for a moment. When he returns it is to find a courting couple (Sunny and another actor) on the bench, locked in a passionate embrace, oblivious to the world. Frankie's efforts to retrieve his lollipop, putting his hand into delicate areas and having it coyly smacked away by the girl who thinks it belongs to her young man, bring in all the hilarious rudery its creator intended. The sketch was purely visual with not a word spoken, and allowed Frankie in his short trousers and school cap to contort his features into every suggestive expression in the book as he vainly tried to rescue his sticky lollipop. The sketch was a gem of innuendo, and went down a treat — although when Frankie first heard the word 'innuendo' applied to him, he arched his eyebrows and asked innocently: 'Innuendo? Isn't that an Italian suppository?'

For Sunny, the musical madness came into her life much later. 'I didn't get to larking about with the piano until 1960,' she recalls. 'And that was only because a producer called up from South Africa inviting Frank to go down there on a tour. They wanted the sketches, and they wanted Frank's act. But they would only send two air tickets.'

Sunny recalls: 'Blanche couldn't go, and Frank was in one of his doldrums financially, not earning very much, so he couldn't afford another accompanist. He said to me: "You've just got to play the piano."'

'I told him: "I can't possibly play for you."'

'He said: "I've heard you play. You can do it — and you *will* do it!" That was Frank. He could charm the birds off the trees if he set his heart on it. So I went with him.'

The tour took in Johannesburg, Capetown, Durban, Pietermaritzburg and on up into Zimbabwe (then Rhodesia) in theatres in Salisbury and Bulawayo. 'He was wonderfully popular, his name had carried across the world.'

But Frankie was a strict task-master. 'I thought I was going mental,' Sunny reveals. 'There was a piano somewhere in every hotel we stayed in, and the first thing I did after checking in was to go prowling around to find it. Then I would get up at six o'clock every morning, take my sheet music down to the restaurant or club or wherever the piano was located, and just sit down and practise by myself before breakfast. I could read music. But there was so much to memorize. And I hadn't played the piano properly since my schooldays. So I just practised and practised until I got it firmly into my head.

'Frank would appear around ten, and we'd go through his act for hour after hour. I never knew such a perfectionist, though I've heard that comedians are like that. Norman Wisdom was another. But Frank was never completely satisfied — he always felt there was this little bit more that could be polished up. By now every "oooh" and "aaah" was choreographed. And my goodness me, I've never been so terrified in all my life!'

Sunny's fears proved groundless. The piano, an essential part of the act, proved its worth — and so did the virtuoso at the keyboard. In fact Sunny is an accomplished musician, so much so that at one club in the north of England she found the piano had been taken away for repairs, and improvised on the spot with a piano accordion! It brought a whole new tone to the act, but Sunny's arms ached for a week.

On that tour in the southern hemisphere she had no idea that she was cutting her teeth for a future career, and would become a unique 'straight man' — as she always called herself — in a business noted for its eccentrics.

'The important thing was that I should appear to be deaf. We were all deaf pianists, all three of us — Madame Roper, Dame Blanche and now me! I would let rip with "Autumn Leaves" and "Three Coins in the Fountain" while Frank just stood by mouthing at me, and making lewd comments. I adored being his "poor old soul!" '

Blanche had been Frankie's long-suffering pianist for more than ten years. 'She took over again after he came home, and I went back to my cowgirl act.' There was plenty of work for Sunny while Frank was off doing his films or plays, but around the late sixties anno domini started to make itself felt. 'Finally I became too old for rope-twirling! But I was able to take over the piano stool in earnest.'

Sunny became Frankie's accompanist full time, appearing with him in theatres, clubs and pantomimes around the country. She was with him in 1958 when the Royal Invitation came to perform at Windsor Castle for the annual staff Christmas party.

Frankie, of course, nearly threw a fit when the gold-edged invitation dropped through his letter-box. He put a frantic call through to Sunny. 'We — we're going to W-W-W- — ' Sunny couldn't think what he was going to say, though it sounded as if it might be rude. But this time the stutter was the genuine article. 'W-Windsor!' he cried. 'Get your skates on, and come round here, sharpish.'

She knew the act off by heart by now, but that wasn't good

enough for her perfectionist master. Frankie had heard that the stage in the historic Waterloo Chamber where he would be performing for the Queen and castle staff was very small, and he worried accordingly.

Where would he stand? How close to the piano could he get without blocking off the audience's view of Sunny? Could they see him from all parts of the Chamber? What about the acoustics — would he get a chance to test them? Oh dear! Frankie would suffer several fitful nights of torment before the appointed hour. He was going to the Waterloo Chamber, not the Bloody Tower, but no one would have known it.

In fact, he was right about the acoustics. The Waterloo Chamber tended to have a slight echo, which could be off-putting for the unwary. And the stage? 'It was tiny,' Sunny recalls.

On the night, when Frankie peered discreetly through the side curtain, Sunny had to hold his arm to stop it trembling. An intimate audience of around three hundred people awaited them, almost the entire castle staff. And in the front row — 'Cor, look? It's the Queen!' Now Frankie was shaking all over. And . . . 'Gawd, it's all of them — '

And it was. All the royals had gathered that Christmas for the traditional staff treat, and young Charles and Anne were excitedly hopping about by the front row in eager anticipation of the show.

'Don't worry, Frank,' Sunny soothed. 'You've done this before. What about the Royal Variety Shows?'

'Yeah,' retorted Frankie, 'But I've never been breathing down me nose at 'em that close in me life!'

True enough. From the Palladium stage the view of the royal box is of a few white blobs in the darkness and the occasional glimpse of a pair of white gloves clapping. And although Frankie had shaken the royal mitt more than once, it had always been as part of a line-up. But now, there they all were, the massed British monarchy. Less than fifteen feet away, three steps down beyond a decorative row of fresh flowers.

Waiting for him . . .

Sunny went out first, curtsied low, and took her seat at the piano with decorum. Out lurched Frankie. Bowed, sort of. Looked around. Took a deep breath.

'Oh! There you are . . . Well . . . er . . . I shan't keep you long

. . . um . . . now . . . how are you? You all right? Me? . . . no, I feel a bit . . . No, listen, I went to the doctor. What's today – Sunday? Yes, no, Monday it was, Monday week . . .?

Already the laughter was building, led by the Queen and Queen Mother in the front row, who had never hidden the fact that they found Frankie a hoot. The Queen Mum especially. The seal of royal approval was stamped on the evening. And Frankie was off and running, the bloodhound features cajoling, pleading, imploring them to understand his plight.

'*No, listen, liss-en . . . In the evening, I went in the evening. I always go to the doctor in the evening, his hands are warm by then . . . no, really . . . Anyway, he said I should take a holiday, so I went down to this travel agent, see . . . Never again, I'll never go there again . . . There was this girl behind the counter. "Excuse me," I said. "Can I see your brochures?" . . . "I beg your pardon?" she said . . .*'

The Waterloo Chamber rocked with hilarity. Nerves completely forgotten, Frankie ploughed on to glory. If the first stutter or two had been for real, the rest were scripted and it was business as usual.

' *"Well then, your tours . . ." And she said: "You're not touring all over my brochures" . . . And I thought to meself: "We've got a right one 'ere for a start! . . ."* '

Sunny, laughing now, remembers the aftermath. 'It was a triumph. Frankie had everyone in stitches. Afterwards we all gathered in a little anteroom to be introduced – and the Queen was just wonderful. She sat down and patted the sofa beside her and said: "Come and sit down!" And she just chatted to us like an old friend. In two minutes flat she had put us both completely at ease. She has that gift, of course, but it's wonderful to experience it at first hand.

'Afterwards, in the car back to London, I said: "What a marvellous evening!" Frankie was completely drained – more from his early nerves than anything else. But as I said to him, "If you don't get butterflies, be careful. You might get too cocky."

'He looked at me with his face still a bit pale, and said: "Cocky? Me? After all I've been through? I don't think you need ever worry about that, dear!" '

Sunny knew there was a dark side to the mooning, and defended it stoutly. 'Isn't there in everybody? People don't like hearing bad things about their idols, they get upset. And I can understand that. Frank had his problems, more than most people. He went through some very bad times. But I want to remember the man I knew and loved as a dear friend. That's all.'

When Frankie hit the bad times, Sunny simply sat back and waited. She couldn't do anything else except offer a shoulder to cry on. He knew she would always be around when the time came to ask her back to the home they shared – a stage large or small, a theatre or club. Sunny herself never married, and had no responsibilities to anyone but herself.

She would be around.

The last time Sunny sat down to the keyboard and waited for Frankie to say 'She's past it, poor old soul!' was in 1990 at the Garrick Theatre with his one-man show.

Eight years previously, Sunny was taken ill with thyroid trouble, and had an emergency operation in St Bartholomew's Hospital in the City of London, ending up in intensive care. She had gone in for a minor op for a cyst on the back of her neck, then complications set in. 'We thought she was going to die,' said her neighbour Alwyn Miller.

Alwyn put the phone down from the hospital, picked it up, and dialled Frankie. She could hear the sounds of a dinner party in full swing in the background. Frankie took the call, heard the details, called the hospital himself and phoned for a taxi to rush him across London to the City. Inside Bart's he stayed an hour watching through the glass window into the Intensive Care Unit until he was assured there was nothing more he could do. Then he went back home to his guests.

'He was so concerned,' said Alwyn. 'I didn't know who else to turn to. But Frank came up trumps.' Sunny came through with all flags flying and the bond of affection between them was all the deeper for it.

She would scold him over his dress sense. Frankie could surprise everyone by appearing as a model of sartorial elegance – then ruin it. The last time she saw it with her own eyes was in the summer of 1990, when they were at the Garrick together. Sunny stayed in town during the week, as a house guest at Frankie's Kensington home.

One morning she came downstairs to the hall and there was Frankie by the front door, resplendent in a dark brown silk suit, crisp shirt and matching tie. 'He looked *gorgeous*,' Sunny remembers. 'I said: "You look absolutely beautiful! Where are you going?"

'He said: "I've got a very important lunch date. Got to look my best."

'I said: "Well, you look lovely." And he really did. He was immaculate.

'After lunch he came back, and I didn't see him again until it was time to go to the theatre. And he must have slept in it! He took an afternoon nap — fully dressed in that suit. It was horribly creased and his shirt was all crumpled. I was horrified.

'I said to Dennis: "Just look at that suit! What has he done to it?"

'Dennis just shrugged. "Well, you know Frank!"

Johnny Mans, himself a former stand-up comedian who became a promoter and agent with the Billy Marsh organization, noticed how Frankie would often turn up in a suit, usually the favourite 'warm' brown or beige, with a pastel-coloured shirt — and no tie. 'I'd keep looking at my watch and say: "Isn't it time you went and changed?" And Frankie would fish in one pocket and pull out a tie, usually patterned in some pale colour.

'He would wander on stage for a few minutes in the first half to let the audience get a look at him, and throw a few gags at them. Then for his main spot in the second half he'd fish in the other pocket and bring out a different tie. It certainly kept his luggage light!' It also contributed to his rumpled image — the bulging jacket pockets, the loose-fitting clothes, and the comfortable air of someone who has dropped by for a gossip over the garden fence.

Sunny smiles reminiscently. 'And he was always like that. You only had to see him on television to realize it. He was the only man I knew who could wear a £750 suit and look super — then sleep in it!'

Away from Frankie's influence, those in the business who know Sunny recognized what her true destiny could and perhaps should have been: as a choreographer. Dancing was her first and last love, though Frankie never knew it. 'People said that if I hadn't been so attached to Frank I could have been another Wendy Toye,' she says with a wry smile. 'I'd like to think that was true.'

Sunny's enduring memory of her Frankie was the last time they spoke – on Good Friday, just two days before his death. And of the laughter they shared that day.

It was 6.30 in the evening, and Sunny was getting ready to greet dinner guests who would be arriving in half an hour. 'The phone rang – and there was Frank's voice on the other end. I shall never forget that conversation.' Sunny's eyes cloud momentarily behind her spectacles. 'We laughed . . . and we laughed . . . and we laughed. We couldn't stop. He was telling me all about the hospital and what it was like in there, having all these tests.

'He said: "I don't know what was going on, Sunny, really I don't. They were poking and prodding me, and I had all these people in white coats bending over me in the operating theatre . . ." ' You can hear his voice saying it.

'He sounded just like the old Frank, and maybe he was giving me a special last performance. We talked for twenty minutes – and that's what I'm going to remember about him. The laughter at the end of our lives together.

'I had no hint that he would be dead within two days. No hint at all. I think we were laughing about the whole silly business of life and death – the what's-it-all-about and why-are-we-here of everything. And for some reason we found it excruciatingly funny.

'I really thought he was going to get better after we talked. But the next thing I knew there was another phone call on Easter Sunday. And I was completely shattered.'

It was Dennis Heymer, the agent who shared Frankie's house. His voice was broken. He said three words: 'He's gone, Sunny . . .'

7

The Spice of Life

Frankie Howerd had sailed into the sights of Bernard Delfont in 1948, a year when he was climbing fast to an early peak in a career that would be a roller-coaster ride through giddy heights to rock bottom troughs of despair. The place was the Shepherd's Bush Empire, an old, atmospheric theatre facing the Green that would later be taken over by the BBC for *Wogan* and other TV shows that needed an audience. The revue was called *Ta-Ra-Ra-Boom-De-Ay*.

It was one of Delfont's earlier sorties as a young, get-up-and-go entrepreneur putting on shows for all the family. He was still licking his wounds over the failure of Yves Montand, the French heart-throb he had brought in specially from Paris, to storm London with a one-man show at the Saville Theatre. The critics loved him. The public looked at the posters – and went on walking. The show collapsed.

Delfont needed a money-spinner, and fast. 'To be honest, I was trying to be an impresario. I'd actually appeared on that same Shepherd's Bush stage as a dancer when I was starting out in the business. The place hadn't changed, even if I had!'

Now he gambled on the public wanting to see Frankie's face. The one to fit to the voice that had them laughing twice a month on *Variety Bandbox*. The vehicle? A revue from the Continent called the *Dutch Folies Bergere*, 'naughty but nice', which he had renamed *Ta-Ra*.

'The audience loved Frankie from the moment he stepped out on the stage,' says Delfont. 'It was an enormous success. Nobody had tumbled to just how popular he was, but everywhere we took that show they just flocked to the theatres.'

That was how it was in the breathless years that followed. Frankie was top of the pile, heading onward and upward. He took his own variety show around the country. At Blackpool a duo named Ted and Barbara Andrews were on the bill, and on the end of the pier was their twelve-year-old daughter Julie, singing her heart out in another variety show with an up-and-coming comic named Norman Wisdom.

It was at the Sheffield Empire in the late forties that Norman and Frankie had found themselves as a pair of unknown funny men jostling for position at the bottom of the ladder. 'It was the only time we ever appeared on the same bill together outside a Royal Variety Show,' Norman recalls. 'We sat in our small dressing-room bolstering each other's confidence before we went out – Frankie was on first half, I was on second.'

'I remember telling him: "You've got a great act. Don't worry so much."'

'He replied: "I can't help it. I worry all the time. Do you think they'll understand me?"'

'Then he went out and knocked them in the aisles.'

It was in 1953 that Frankie fell out with his agent in a public and bitter row. His relations with Jack Payne had been growing strained as the months went on, and after six years matters came to a head in the High Court. Both of them alleged breach of contract.

Court No. 6 in the Queen's Bench Division in the Strand was packed when the case began on 19 March. People crowded in to stand three deep to watch the drama unfold. Behind the glass-panelled swing doors, the players sat on rows of hard seats as the curtain went up on what one observer called 'The Show Without a Laugh – Almost!' The source of what little humour there was appeared to be the judge. Mr Justice Hilbery, impressive in black robe, tight belt, ermine cuffs and red sash, was heard to remark apropos of nothing: 'I have yet to meet anyone who would not have gone many times to see Dan Leno.'

The grandest of music hall Dames would no doubt have been flattered, but Frankie found little to laugh at. He sat solemn and expressionless, biting his nails, rubbing his face. The brightest thing about him was his tie. Jack Payne doodled with a silver pencil for much of the time, but was impelled to rise to his feet at one point and wave his horn-rimmed spectacles in anger to protest: 'Sir, you are suggesting I am a thief and a liar. I emphatically deny that on my oath.'

The issues were summed up. For Frankie: 'To right the wrong

done me.' And for Payne: 'My honour and integrity.'

Riveting stuff, worthy of a TV special if not quite a soap, and it filled several column inches of the papers for a week before the verdict. Frankie had retained a flamboyant barrister in the weighty shape of Gilbert Beyfus QC, while the rival legal eagle who would make his name was Fearnley Whittingstall.

Frankie won. He was awarded £5,216, a sum which sounds staggeringly modest by today's inflated figures. But he was happy with it, particularly as Payne's counter-claim was dismissed. The agent lodged an appeal, but long before the October date set for the hearing they settled out of court, with only the legal costs involved. Honours uneasily even. The pair never spoke again.

One sign that you were on top of the world as a comic was to be invited to take part in the Royal Variety Performance, the most prestigious live show in the year, with proceeds going to the Entertainment Artistes' Benevolent Fund. The charity supports Brinsworth House, the peaceful retirement home for elderly performers in Twickenham, besides helping thousands of artistes from the circus, cabaret and clubs as well as from the stage, TV and radio.

The show itself has been blessed by the monarch of the day ever since its first airing on 1 July 1912 at the Palace Theatre, Shaftesbury Avenue, in the presence of King George V and Queen Mary. In the words of its honorary chairman Roy Hudd: 'It is the great accolade − and certainly the most nerve-racking gig a performer will ever tackle.'

Frankie Howerd's nerves were at full jangle when he got the call in 1950. The date: 13 November. The place: The London Palladium. And the guests: King George VI and Queen Elizabeth, later to become known to her subjects as the Queen Mum and to be the Royal Show's most regular visitor. 'There is no real pecking order in a royal show,' says Norman Wisdom, who has had his share of them. 'Everyone is equal on that night.'

That night the dressing-rooms were crowded with a glittering array of talent: singers like Gracie Fields and Donald Peers, comedians like Max Miller, Flanagan and Allen leading the Crazy Gang, Max Bygraves, Tommy Trinder and Max Wall, with Jack

Benny and Dinah Shore brought in from across the Atlantic for a spot of 'Hands across the Sea' camaraderie.

Tommy Trinder was given the unenviable task of warming up the audience before the arrival of the royal party. As Lord Delfont, the Life President of the Benevolent Fund and host for the event, would put it: 'He had to cajole the notoriously unresponsive audience into life.' The amiable Trinder did so, largely thanks to the Crazy Gang who materialized in the royal box dressed as cleaners, throwing out old programmes and assorted litter on to the distinguished heads below.

It was an intimidating night for any comic facing his first royal show. Frankie had been in the public eye for close to five years – but entertainers with a lifetime of experience had been known to quail when faced with the white gloves in the red velvet box less than thirty feet away.

And he died the death.

Afterwards everyone blamed the running order, because the act Frankie had to follow was the brash Billy Cotton Band whose leader's stentorian war cry of 'Wakey, *Wakey*!' was the fifties equivalent of heavy metal. They ended with the band hurling balls of cotton wool into the audience while Billy bellowed out the unlovely refrain of 'I've Got a Luvverly Bunch of Coconuts', a finale that was designed to degenerate into a pitched battle. Cultural it was not. But an approving handful of cotton wool balls even came back from the royal box, to a renewed burst of cheering.

After which poor Frankie had to emerge from the wings, a lone figure who reminded at least one onlooker of a goat tethered to a tree as bait for the next pride of lions passing that way.

His nerves had been in shreds anyway – though for once, backstage, he was in good company. And for eight minutes Frankie stuttered and stammered and ooh-ed and aah-ed to the second worst sound in the world for a comic – just the odd polite titter here and there. The worst, of course, being stony silence. Or maybe a boo. In Frankie's own words: 'I had the impact of a drizzle following a typhoon.'

When mercifully he came off at last, Frankie took to the streets. He trudged around Soho in his raincoat and hat like a lost soul, unable to face anyone backstage, until the time came when he was forced to return for the finale. He lined up to meet the royal guests, but could never remember afterwards what they said to him, if anything. And he felt so ashamed he ducked the big party, and went quietly home. Not one of his best nights, but at least the critics were kind — they didn't mention him at all! And impresario Val Parnell would assure him later: 'It wasn't as bad as you thought.'

To prove that all was forgiven and forgotten, Frankie was invited back again a number of times — as well as giving that very special performance at Windsor Castle. His name was officially listed on the glossy, gold-covered programmes in 1954, 1960 and again in 1966. In fact he would also appear without any warning, just as those other two pranksters Morecambe and Wise did when an act called Marvo and Dolores turned out to be Eric and Ernie.

It was in the 1968 show that the Supremes, backing Diana Ross, scandalized the audience by giving a clenched-fist Black Power salute as they took their bow. Diana, mindful of the assassination that year of civil rights leader Martin Luther King, had paid her own tribute to him in the middle of singing 'Somewhere'. The Queen Mother was in the royal box. At the day-long rehearsals the producer Robert Nesbitt warned the black group not to give any provocative gestures on this special occasion. But the fists went up.

As the Supremes made their whooping exit, Frankie appeared unannounced, watched them go, then shrugged and said: 'That was a bit political, wasn't it? I thought I'd come to the wrong place.' Extra cheer for Francis. The Supremes put in their place. And the audience won back into good humour.

It was Frankie's idea not to be billed. 'It was at his own request,' Delfont reveals. ' "Let's surprise 'em," he'd say to me. "I'll just walk out and see what happens." '

In fact, he had seen George Raft do the same thing on the same stage — appearing unexpectedly from the wings, standing, letting the applause die away . . . before fishing into one pocket and producing a coin. Like the one he tossed in *Scarface*, the classic 1932 gangster movie with Paul Muni and Boris Karloff, where Raft threw the coin in the air repeatedly, and always caught it. The trick was that he didn't actually look at it. This time he strolled on, pulled out the coin, flicked it into the air. And dropped it! Then he snapped his fingers in disgust – and walked off. Not a word was said . . . and the cheers could be heard as far as Oxford Circus.

Frankie knew all about the surprise factor. And at the Royal Variety Shows he milked it for all it was worth. Which is why his name has appeared on the programme rather less often than he appeared on the stage.

What happened, predictably, was an instant hum of recognition . . . then a cheer . . . then thunderous applause, before Francis had even opened his mouth. Usually he would start off in the time-honoured manner: *'I seem to have lost me way. Oh, hullo! –'* A furtive glance at the white gloves resting on the balcony of the royal box, and Frankie was away.

'It worked marvellously without announcing him,' says Delfont. 'You could hear the buzz, then the crescendo. He was very astute about what he wanted to do, and when to do it.'

The famous running gag about 'Thing' upstairs actually took Bernard Delfont by surprise. It was in 1960 and a decade had passed since Frankie's first disastrous effort. The Queen Mum was present again, loyal to the cause as ever. Sitting in his front row seat below the royal box, Bernie watched as Frankie ambled out on stage, gestured upstairs to a fictitious office, and said: *'It's Thing . . . You know. His name's – well, I forget 'is name. But he owns the place.'*

Then, behind his cupped hand in a hissed aside! *'Common as muck!'* It became the hit of the show, the line they all talked about afterwards. In fact Frankie referred to anyone in authority as 'Thing', and it had already become part of his vocabulary.

But on this particular night he went even further, pointing up at the elaborate floral arrangement around the royal box. *'Carnations,'* he confided. *'Hundreds of 'em. "Thing" did it all himself, y'know. Personally. He was up all night. Oh yes . . . Why? Because last year he got someone else to do it and found one carnation missing.'* Sympathetic letters dropped into the Delfont office complaining that Frankie should not be allowed to say such awful things. Insulting the boss? Well, since the boss had a sense of humour and laughed louder than anyone – why not?

Word was hastily put around by worried minions that the star had cleared every word of it with his future Lordship. Not so. Later, yes, when people — including the royal party — actually started to expect Delfont to be sent up from the stage.

Today Delfont still chuckles at it, sitting in his office overlooking Soho Square. 'I kept some of those letters. They said things like: "I think it's disgraceful the way you allow this . . ." I must admit I was taken aback the first time. But after that Frankie would come into my office several weeks before the big night, and show me the script he planned to do. I always said: "That's fine, Frank. Whatever you want to say — go right ahead!" And I never altered a word. I was a good butt for him on the royal night out.'

Frankie would regale friends with the story of how he was rehearsing the 1967 Royal Command Performance at the Palladium.

His own favourite tipple was gin and tonic, with wine over meals. Later it would become vodka. Unlike his good friend Tommy Cooper, who had a reputation for going on stage with a skinful under his belt, Frankie was meticulous about his alcoholic intake before a show — although later there would be the occasional lapse. Indeed, when poor Tommy Cooper keeled over on stage with Jimmy Tarbuck in front of millions of TV viewers and was dragged under the curtain and out of sight, most of those who knew him thought the big man had simply had one too many.

Frankie had a soft spot for Tommy, another household favourite who left an irreplaceable gap when he passed on. The show traditionally was on a Monday. On the Sunday before, as usual, rehearsals began in the morning and went on all day and far into the night until they got it the way the director, Robert Nesbitt, wanted it.

'I was on after Tommy,' recalled Frankie. 'I knew he'd been on the sauce a little more than was good for him. I was due to be on at the end. We'd all been going sixteen hours non-stop — sitting around in the stalls when we weren't wanted, watching the other acts, chatting among ourselves.

'Bob Nesbitt shouted: "Next act!" — which was Tommy. We

could hear Tommy going through his act . . . but the curtain hadn't moved. When they finally pulled the drapes aside, there was Tommy, practically legless, doing the full number − but facing the backcloth!

'Tommy turns round, sees us all gawping at him, swallows and says: "Oh, Bob − oh" − (in a brilliant take-off of Tommy, remember Frankie used to be an impressionist) − "Oh, Bob, I'm terribly sorry . . ."'

'But Bob said: "Is he pissed?"'

'We all chorused: "Yes, he's pissed!"'

'And Bob said: "Well, sober him up and tell him to keep doing it! It's wonderful." '

And that's what Tommy Cooper did next night. Keeping the act going to a pitch-black rear curtain, finally realizing from the laughter that perhaps he was facing north when it should be south, turning to look up at the royal box in relief, and announcing: 'I thought it was a bit empty for a Monday!'

Tommy would keep that gag in his act and it would always get a laugh. Some comics are funny whichever way they're facing − Frankie Howerd was another, as Francis proved with his dramatic exit from the Oxford Union debating society in 1991 − in a white smock with a slit up the back to expose the Howerd nether regions in all their dubious glory.

Frankie Howerd saw the inside of most of the big variety theatres around the country, either with his own show or in pantomime. His reputation as a stickler for perfection was matched only by his other reputation − for clumsiness. It was nourished by such incidents as the one that happened at the Winter Garden, Bournemouth, in the fifties, when Frankie was rehearsing *Alice in Wonderland*. He managed to knock a fellow actor off the stage and into the orchestra pit, and the next day measured his length on the boards after sitting back on a table that a stagehand had removed thirty seconds earlier.

The trail led inevitably and triumphantly to the West End, and the Palladium. In 1950 Frankie starred in *Out of This World*, and was back in time for Christmas in *Dick Whittington*, playing Idle Jack, and heading a cast of household favourites like Jerry Desmonde as his stooge, Richard Hearn (Mr Pastry) and Sonny

Hale. In 1953 Bernard Delfont put him into the Prince of Wales with Winifred Atwell in a spectacular revue called *Pardon My French*, suitably peppered with statuesque topless showgirls, in which Frankie was ably assisted by Lee Young and the devoted Madam Sunny Rogers at the keyboard. It was another winner, running for over a year.

During his lifetime, Frankie was lucky enough to have some marvellous scripts to back him. His proud boast was that 'Most of the famous writers have written for me at some time.' And it was true, they had. 'Oh yes,' he would say airily, before dropping a few choice names. 'Galton and Simpson, Hills and Green, Johnny Speight, Eric Sykes, Muir and Norden. All gratefully received.'

He had inherited Galton and Simpson after their huge success with *Steptoe and Son*. 'Alan and Ray are good lads. I like to help them, poor devils. They've been writing for a couple of rag and bone men, you know. It's such a thrill for them to be back working for the gentry . . .'

It was this redoubtable pair who wrote another West End hit around Frankie, *Way Out in Piccadilly*, a lively revue directed by Eric Sykes, which starred him with Cilla Black, enjoying her own heady success as top of the pops. The combination was irresistible, and the show ran for almost two years, featuring such gems of subtlety as: 'I will now perform a number by Rippernikersoff.'

The one time Frankie and Cilla faltered during the long run was when they heard that Richard Burton and Elizabeth Taylor were in the audience. So was the entourage – 'the Circus', as it was called – that accompanied them everywhere in those headline-grabbing jet-setting days before show business's most famous marriage fell apart for the second time.

Frankie peered through a slit in the curtain. Sure enough, a large slice of the fifth row was taken up by the show business 'royals' and their courtiers.

He felt his knees go to jelly. It had happened countless times before, though not when a show was going as well as this one. But, as he would explain: 'It's extraordinary how really terrified you get if other artists in the profession are watching you. And the more famous they are – the worse it is. Olivier would send tremors through an entire cast if they knew he was out front.'

Burton and Taylor were in town for the royal film performance of *The Taming of the Shrew* at the Odeon, Leicester Square, less than a hundred yards from the Prince of Wales. They stayed on at the Dorchester, their habitual hangout when in London, and Burton remembered seeing the posters for Frankie's show on the way to the royal screening. He also recalled blowing his own trumpet on Frankie's radio show — a story with which he had regaled Liz more than once.

Cilla's reaction when Frankie told her the news didn't help, either. 'Oh, God!' she exclaimed, and started to tremble visibly.

Both their performances were affected. Frankie's timing was off. Cilla sang flat. But neither Burton not Liz appeared to notice.

They came backstage afterwards, and Richard's opening words were: 'Nice to see you again. Great show!' while Liz compounded the praise by saying loudly: 'Did anyone ever tell you that you're the funniest man in the world? If they didn't, I'm telling you now!' It was music to Frankie's eager ears.

The Burtons insisted on celebrating the reunion with dinner at their hotel. Nothing loath, his nerves in temporary suspension, Frankie embarked on a night on the town that would leave him with a hangover, and a memory he would treasure all his days. Steak and kidney pud (the Francis favourite) in the Grill Room at the Dorchester. Then a chauffeur-driven Rolls Royce to Annabel's, the basement dive haunted by the rich and famous in Berkeley Square. For a bonus: a dance with Liz Taylor, still in her eye-catching prime. That was one sore head worth nursing, he decided the next day.

Also worth nursing, in 1972, was the memory of Elizabeth Taylor's fortieth birthday party, when the Circus took up temporary residence in Budapest. To his surprise Frankie found himself an honoured guest, sharing the top table with the likes of Princess Grace, Michael Caine, Ringo Starr, Raquel Welch and other luminaries invited by the Burtons in their insatiable quest for headlines. Frankie's main memory of a vodka-shrouded weekend was being stuck in a lift with Raquel Welch. 'I was quite sorry when they got it started again,' he told the assembled masses from the world's Press.

8

The Other Women . . .

If Sunny Rogers was Frankie Howerd's surrogate wife, the other woman in his life was Jeanne Mockford. Unknown and unsung, she was his friend and confidante, sharing a laugh one day, providing a shoulder to cry on the next. An attractive, auburn-haired actress twenty years his junior with a vivacious personality, Jeanne first met Frankie in 1956 – and became an integral part of his life.

She played Senna (as in Pods) in *Up Pompeii*, her most memorable line being to shriek out: 'Woe, woe is me . . .' The daughter of a bank clerk from South London, RADA-trained, she came up through repertory and finally found herself on a stage with Frankie in Carlisle during a charity evening. He was in excerpts from *Charley's Aunt*, she was touring in a series of playlets.

'We hit it off from the word go. Call it chemistry,' she says. Frankie went on to Bromley to appear in *Tons of Money* with Sheila Hancock, and called her up to invite her to join the cast. Jeanne would become one of the inner circle of Frankie's bosom friends, holidaying with him in Malta and staying as a house guest at his Somerset cottage.

'I've got so many memories of him. The good times – and the bad. He was such a mixed-up person. But so kind and caring. If anybody was ill he'd be round to see them like a shot. Yet he would always say: "Nobody will care after I've died . . ." It was so untrue . . .'

Jeanne, young and vibrant, was given the second lead, the beautiful ingénue flirting with Frankie throughout the two-hour farce. From Bromley, *Tons of Money* took off round the country and Jeanne recalls how on stage he would mutter out of the corner of his mouth: 'Coming out for a drink afterwards?' 'He was doing everything he could to make me "corpse" – and he would succeed! He was always being outrageous.'

Going out for a drink could prove dangerous. 'Frank never

forgot the time I passed out in the gent's loo at Nottingham Playhouse on New Year's Eve. He was always pulling my leg. But I don't remember a thing about it!'

The inner circle of Frankie's show biz lady friends consisted of Jeanne, Cilla Black, June Whitfield, Sunny Rogers, Margaret Courtenay and Barbara Windsor.

'Frank used to throw the most wonderful parties,' Jeanne recalls. 'The same people were always there. Plus Richard Burton and Zsa Zsa Gabor if they were in the country. Quite often Frankie would lead us all into a "Knees Up Mother Brown". I used to do the cooking for him. He was totally hopeless in the kitchen. All he could do was make a cup of coffee – and that was an effort!'

One kind of food was off limits: 'He couldn't eat onions or garlic. It gave him dyspepsia. And of course it's very difficult when you're trying to cook a nice meal *not* to use onions or garlic . . .

' "It gives me wind, darling!" he would say.'

They also shared a mutual, almost obsessive concern over their health. 'I'm a hypochondriac, too! We'd be on the phone for hours, talking about our ailments! He would go on and on.' Keep taking the tablets, they'd tell each other before the phone went down . . .

Jeanne was firm on one score: 'I never indulged his moods. I would be terribly school ma'am-ish with him, and jolly him out of it.' And on another – Frankie's gambling habits. 'We used to spend hours playing nap, but I insisted on small stakes!'

Jeanne lived less than two minutes' walk from Frankie's home in Edwardes Square, so it was no real surprise when he would ring her up out of the blue and invite her out to dinner. Jeanne did not worry about exactly what would happen. It all depended on Frankie's mood – whether the evening would be pure pleasure – or whether she would want to crawl under the table in embarrassment.

'Frankie could be so outrageous in the things he would say to people, it was quite dreadful. Like waiters: He would always ask them about their sex life, and if they were getting enough of it. *"Did you score last night, then?"* Or, worse, at an Italian restaurant, if they were in the Mafia!'

'I would say: "Frank, you can't *do* that!" But, of course, he did.

'He loved to shock people. He had a wicked sense of humour.'

Jeanne saw Francis flare up more times than she can remember. Usually it was over and done with in a moment — 'But he could be pretty devastating. The smallest thing could trigger it off.'

Frankie loathed noise, 'it would drive him up the wall.' He would go to bed and get up late, and if his beauty sleep was disturbed he would let the world know it in no uncertain terms. Particularly in the country, at his cottage near Axbridge, Somerset. 'We had to creep around the house until he came down for lunch, not run the taps too hard, and not pull the loo chain. As for taking a shower — I couldn't even have that on full blast! The rule of house was that you had to be quiet. Very quiet. Frankie would get very upset.

'I get up early, so I had to make sure I walked around on tiptoe. No high heels on the staircase! He would go to bed at 2.00 a.m., sometimes later.' Old habits die hard in the theatre. 'He would tell you: Either phone him at half-past twelve in the daytime or half-past twelve at night. Never, but never, in the morning.'

Jeanne admits: 'I'm not terribly good late at night. I'm more of a morning person.' Nevertheless, she indulged Frankie's whims for late card sessions, often extending into an all-night gambling den — albeit for modest stakes. 'Often I would watch the sun come up,' she recalls.

Jeanne has a personal experience of Frankie's generosity which she treasures: one year she was 'resting' for five months and Frankie offered to pay her a weekly wage, as if she was in work. Jeanne refused — but he insisted. And within three weeks a job came along for her. But she never forgot the gesture of a kind and generous friend.

Behind the scenes Frankie's kindness was legendary, but very private. He never advertised the gifts he donated to charity, or the helping hand he gave to friends in trouble. Or the caring. Mrs Tommy Cooper — Dove to her friends — would always cook him his favourite steak and kidney pudding when he came to dinner at their Chiswick home. 'He was one of the very few people who phoned me up after Tommy died,' she recalls. 'He was just a lovely man.'

*

Vivacious actress Margaret Courtenay became one of Frankie's close chums after − as she put it − 'seeing his Bottom' in *A Midsummer Night's Dream*. As one of the respected Old Vic family, she viewed the impending arrival of the stuttering comic with mixed feelings. Like the rest of the company, Maggie (who played Hippolata) wasn't at all sure if it was − well, a *good idea* to unleash Francis on the hallowed boards across Waterloo Bridge.

'We were a little apprehensive, yes we were,' she admitted afterwards, with the echoes of the laughter and applause still singing in the rafters. 'But we needn't have worried for a single moment. When we first heard he had been signed, someone said: "Ah, Frankie's going to show us his Bottom!" And all the jokes went on from there.

'But when he arrived at the theatre on the first day of rehearsals, he was word perfect. He knew every line − and most of ours, too. And not a single "oooh" or "aaaah" did we hear throughout the entire production. He never mucked about − but he was still terribly funny. He simply couldn't help it.'

Maggie lived across Edwardes Square at No. 17, while Frankie was at No. 27. 'It was known as Faggots' Row,' she recalls, one eyebrow arched in mock horror. 'There were an enormous number of actors in that square, from Ian McKellen to Peter Wyngarde, and loads more. It was like a club. We would all meet in the gardens walking our dogs or just out for a stroll, and we'd catch up with all the latest gossip. I would often pass Frankie heading out towards the High Street with his string bag over one arm, moaning about having to do the shopping. And he was always cadging a lift off me.'

Maggie would look forward to their games of tennis on Sunday afternoons on the old grass court hidden away behind the tree-lined railings of the square. 'Frankie wasn't actually terribly *good*,' she confided. 'Enthusiastic, yes. But I always beat him. He was a very good sport, though, and kept coming back for more.

'He ran about the court like mad, in over-long shorts, and he held his racquet like a frying-pan − absolutely flat! when he served he would shout: "One − two − three −" then throw the ball in the air and whack it. As often as not it sailed past my ear and didn't touch the ground before hitting the wire netting! The court didn't help. The grass was uneven, all tumpty and tufty and daft . . .'

The joke in June Whitfield's household was that Frankie Howerd fell in love with her dog. It is a friendly pooch, a cross between a Tibetan terrier and a Jack Russell, who goes by the curious name of Rabbit — and on occasion when June visited Frankie in the West Country, was known to make a half-hearted effort to chase one. Francis had always been an animal lover. Witness his devotion to his boxer dog Red — 'as amiable and slobbery as myself!' he would say. He and Rabbit got on splendidly when Frankie in turn dropped by June's home in Wimbledon.

They met at Chichester when he was Simple Simon in the pantomime *Jack and the Beanstalk* and June played a fairy. 'We strangled a duet together,' she remembers. 'It was "Spread a Little Happiness" — and didn't he give a lot of it?' After that she featured on numerous TV shows, where he would greet her in front of the rest of the cast and crew with a noisy: 'Oh Gawd! Not 'er!'

Of all his ladies, bubbly Barbara Windsor, clothed or otherwise, was always most associated with the wicked side of Frankie, through *Up Pompeii* and the *Carry On* farces, where she had become one of the stalwarts. Whenever they wanted someone to lose a bra or pop a button, the *Carry On* gang looked no further than Barbara.

In the ten years between 1964–74, Barbara made nine *Carry Ons*. And despite her screen persona, here was one screen bimbo with brains! Born in 1937, the perky daughter of a Shoreditch bus conductor was a bright pupil at school, and it was left to her parents, ambitious for their daughter to taste the bright lights, to push her towards the stage. She first trod the boards in local pantomime. Her mother used up all her own savings to send Barbara to the famous Ada Foster school for young talent, where the tutors were misguided enough to try to iron out her Cockney accent.

But her mum's investment proved a wise one. Barbara, a pocket dynamo in four-inch heels, was spotted by Joan Littlewood, the independent stage director who would give her the role that changed her young life: as pert Rosie in *Fings Ain't Wot They Used t'Be*. At seventeen, Barbara had been one of the gymslip terrors in *The Belles of St Trinian's*, but it was the high-spirited 1963 East End comedy *Sparrows Can't Sing* that hooked her into the *Carry On* net.

Producer Peter Rogers spotted her in the show, and knew he need look no further for the sexpot he wanted to symbolize all that was naughty and doubly-meaningful in his screen romps.

Frankie and Barbara got on famously. They met at Pinewood Studios early in 1968 when Frankie made his first foray into the minefield of bad jokes and worse puns in *Carry On Doctor*, the fourteenth in the series. Alternative titles bandied around that made him emit that short bark of a laugh included 'Where There's a Pill There's a Way' and 'The Bowels are Ringing'. The *Carry On* team had returned to the world of bed-pans, over-long syringes and enemas in an enthusiastic effort to capture the high spirits of *Carry On Nurse* — the one with the unforgettable final scene with James Robertson Justice as the fearsome senior surgeon left lying on his face on the bed with a daffodil planted where a thermometer should be.

Frankie was cast as a certain Francis Bigger, a faith healer, and one of his better lines called for him to flinch as a nurse approaches his bed with a bunch of daffodils, and to cry: 'Oh no you don't. Not that! I saw that film —'

Barbara played a nurse — inevitably popping out of her uniform. Oddly enough, the two were never in front of the camera together, though you would have thought that Frankie's leer could hardly have alighted on a more suitable victim.

But they shared lunches together in the panelled restaurant, and struck up a firm friendship that would endure until his death.

'He could be dreadfully moody, but he was a lovely guy,' says Barbara, back in harness for the 1992 summer show *What a Carry On in Blackpool*. 'We had a million laughs, and we were always insulting each other. On that first meeting he asked me if I had a sleeping pill he could take when he went home that night. Sometimes he couldn't get to sleep at all.

'When I said I had, he raised those great eyebrows of his and cried: "Oooh, with all the men in your life I wouldn't think you needed one!" Subtlety was never Frankie's strong point.'

But the woman who really stole Frankie Howerd's heart was a screen goddess with seductive grey eyes, a peaches-and-cream complexion and a husky voice that had the texture of rich velvet. Joan Greenwood was a strikingly good-looking actress, born under the same sign as Frankie, the daughter of Chelsea artist Sydney Earnshaw Greenwood. In the fifties she starred in Ealing comedies like *The Man in the White Suit*, but was best known for such films as *Whisky Galore* and, particularly, for her most famous role, the marvellous sugary-voiced Gwendolen in the classic 1952 comedy *The Importance of Being Earnest*.

Frankie met her on one of his early radio shows – and flipped. Here was a woman who brought out all the latent tenderness and generosity in him, someone on whom he could lavish his inner dreams and maybe make them come true. They were together for several years, though living apart. And then she suddenly married the eminent classical actor André Morell, leaving Frankie her devoted slave on the sidelines, stunned by what had happened.

Laugh, clown, laugh? Not easy, if the clown is in love. Frankie finally broke his silence on this most private area of his emotions after Joan died in 1987, at the age of sixty-seven. 'I was devoted to Joan. She was a very beautiful girl and we were very close,' he revealed. And, sadly: 'I would like to have married her, but it was not to be. I don't know what went wrong between us, or why it happened. I was saddened and puzzled. I didn't know what had hit me.'

Frankie was talking about his feelings of thirty years before, but somehow making clear they had never faded. 'I didn't see her again,' he ended simply. 'Our paths never crossed. She just went away.'

Surprise, surprise! One of Frankie's closest friends was Cilla Black, pop singer turned queen of the TV game shows. The one-time 'mobile carrot', as she was known at school, struck up a friendship with the comedian during the 1966 stage spectacular *Way Out in Piccadilly*. The show ran for 408 performances at the Prince of Wales. Their friendship lasted a lifetime.

At first Frankie was concerned whether a pop star who had found overnight fame and had a huge following of her own would fit into his show. It was only two years before that Cilla's second single 'Anyone Who Had a Heart' had sold 100,000 copies in one day, and she was at the height of that great wave of popularity which gave her sixteen records in the Top Thirty chart in ten years. 'Not bad for a one-time typist who earned seven pound ten shillings a week,' Frankie said.

He need not have worried. The pair hit it off from the start, largely thanks to the fact that Cilla found Frankie 'hysterical' and could not quench that shrill, infectious giggle that became her trademark.

In turn Frankie became a frequent visitor at the singer's elegant house set in seventeen acres of Buckinghamshire countryside. She and her husband Bobby Willis, who was a baker when he met her but became her manager in 1967, even called Frankie the 'surrogate' godfather to their three sons – Robert, born in 1970, Ben, three years later, and Jack, who came along seven years after that.

'Dear Frankie,' Cilla recalls. 'He was a dear, dear friend. He would always be popping over on the spur of the moment, usually at the weekend. I cook a traditional roast for Sunday lunch. The phone would ring and Frankie would be saying: "Have you put the joint in yet?"

'If I said "No" – he would say: "Right, save it till later because I'm coming over this evening!" '

Frankie not only made Cilla laugh till her sides ached, he also taught her the A–Z of comedy. 'Particularly timing, and he was a master, wasn't he?' she says now. 'Just being with him was a real education, both on and off stage. In that first show, which ran for sixty-eight weeks, I learned so much from him that I've never, ever forgotten. Even today I bring a lot of what Frankie taught me into my TV shows when I've got something funny to say.'

In the mid sixties Frankie hired a new agent. Beryl Vertue had been a typist with his script agency in the old Shepherd's Bush days, and had gone on to bigger and better things. A dynamic, resolute woman who brooked no nonsense from anyone, she had a reputation for driving hard bargains for her clients — and making sure they earned every penny of the considerable money she found for them. Frankie always said she was one of 'my guardian angels'. She in turn could recall how he used to visit her home, play with her children, and bring laughter into her house. And she remembered one remark he would make when discussing fees: 'Shall we say I feel less *turbulent* now than I did before . . .'

Beryl Vertue also has memories of solemn conferences which her client would suddenly interrupt by pointing across the table at her and screeching to whoever sat next to him: 'A slut, that's what she is! Oooh, a terrible slut. Don't take any notice of her name . . .'

With Frankie, once they became a friend, no one was safe.

Tessa Le Bars was his agent for more than two decades, replacing Roger Hancock and Beryl Vertue — who had guided Frankie since the Jack Payne saga. A sturdy, bustling woman with close-cropped red hair and bright hazel eyes, Tessa was Frankie's other mother hen, cluckingly protective against all intruders who sought to invade the coop.

He always called her Tess-*a*, with a loud emphasis on the final 'a'. Four floors above Queen Anne Street, surrounded by the expensive consulting-rooms of Harley and Wigmore Streets, her office is a single room looking out over the roof-tops of Marylebone. She could actually see the slates of the Harley Street Clinic two streets away where her star client would be fighting for his life during that terrible and dramatic April week in 1992.

Frankie liked that room. Pinned on the door was a poster of his one-man show at the Garrick, May 1990, the last he would ever give to a West End audience. ('Plus Madame Rogers at the Piano. Limited run, three weeks only.') Inside, the room was as rumpled and untidy and homely as Frankie himself, papers strewn over the large desk, potted plants waving green fronds from various corners, even an old gas fire opposite a large oil painting of Ray Galton and Alan Simpson dominating the wall above the lumpy sofa. ('We shared the cost, then couldn't decide who should have it,' said Alan. As referee and arbiter, their agent Tessa agreed to hold on to it until the boys made their decision. She has had it ever since.)

Framed photographs on the walls reflect the happy times with Frankie. The first nights. The awards. Frankie surrounded by celebrities. Frankie actually smiling. Frankie clutching his OBE. The days of fun and frolic.

'Frankie was such a huge part of my life,' Tessa says, sifting through papers, programmes, the paraphernalia of the past. 'He was everything to me, and I like to think I was everything to him. A shoulder to lean on, to cry on, to laugh on. I can still hear his voice. "Tess-*a*!" Every time I walk in here I can hear it . . .'

The other shoulder that Frankie needed to know was always there belonged to his sister Betty. His most devoted friend and fan, she still lives less than half a mile from the house in Arbroath Road where they played together as children. Her home is a pebble-dash semi with red Spanish tiles, half-way up Eltham Hill, neat as a new pin, with a pleasant garden. Outside the front gate is a large expanse of grass created by the new roundabout system that thankfully for Betty and her neighbours sends the main coastal traffic trundling off into the distance.

She became Mrs Betty Paye, but the marriage ended – and the only man in her life was her beloved brother. It was with Betty that Frankie had a last dinner-for-two at their favourite restaurant in Kensington High Street, just forty-eight hours before he died on that 1992 Easter Sunday.

And it was Betty, indefatigable and optimistic, who would urge him out of his blackest moods.

'There were times when he wanted anonymity,' she could recall. 'But if anyone asked him: "What do you do for a living?" he would be mortified!'

Very few women outside the immediate coterie of his sister Betty, Cilla, Jeanne and Tessa Le Bars enjoyed the privilege of being seen on Frankie's arm in public. One who did was wardrobe designer Joan Ellacott, who would make sure all the buttons were in the right place on his costume when he filmed *Jumping for Joy* in the winter of 1955. She recalls how they were on location at the White City when Frankie came up to her, and after a few moments' hesitation blurted out: 'Joan, would you come out with me tonight?'

She was taken aback. 'Well, I'll have to ask my husband,' she said.

'That's all right,' said Frankie. 'Go ahead and ask him. But I really would like you to have dinner with me and see a show.'

With some surprise — and with hubby's approval — Joan got herself ready. She left Frankie in the lounge of her West London home while she put the final touches to her make-up, but couldn't help seeing him staring fixedly at his reflection in the antique mirror in the hall, continually teasing and adjusting the curls on top of his forehead.

Carry On producer Peter Rogers was one of many who wondered about Frankie's hairstyle. 'I could never understand why Frankie couldn't spend a little more money to get a different piece of hair,' he said. 'He had the same rug on throughout all the years I knew him.

'And the mirror — that was a nervous thing with him. He couldn't pass a mirror without looking into it and flicking his hair back.' Window-shopping must have been agony!

In fact the talk among fellow comics was that Frankie had the same wig on the day he died as he had worn back in 1947. The truth is that fresh-tonsored or not, Frankie suffered from the condition known medically as alopecia areata (for Latin students: *alopecia*; for Greek students: *alopekia*). This was a bald patch above his forehead about the size of a small saucer, which developed in his early twenties. He was no Yul Brynner, that was for sure, but he was extremely sensitive about that bare circle of scalp — and even had a second assistant fired off a picture at Pinewood Studios when the lad walked into his dressing-room without knocking and found Frankie there, minus his hairpiece.

'His top-knot was off and he was absolutely livid to be discovered like that,' says director Gerald Thomas. 'The story was the talk of the studio for days.' Blowing his top — or top-knot — was so unlike the Frankie Howerd everyone knew and loved that it shook the studio down to its communal boots.

Frankie's tonsorial sensitivity spilled over into the actual making of *Carry On Doctor*. For one scene he was required to be sitting up in bed in the ward, while a nurse pulled his white operating gown up and over his head.

Frankie took his director to one side, and said urgently: 'Gerry, could we have the gown cut so I don't have to pull it over my head? I just want to slide out of it — '

Gerald Thomas, as usual, was polite but firm. 'Sorry, Frankie, it has to be lifted off.'

In the end — compromise. 'I had to film it as it started to come off, says Gerald. 'Then cut to his face, then show the gown already off. He was worried his hairpiece might come off with it — so I went along with him.'

Jean Mockford confirms: 'Frankie was terribly sensitive about his hairpiece. That was something I never, ever mentioned to him in all the years I knew him. Not once. I would never even admit I knew about it . . . however angry I got with him!'

Joan Ellacott continued the story of her night out with Frankie: 'He was very shy. I found I had made up a foursome, and we met another couple at the Café de Paris to see Lena Horne. We had the best table, the best wine, the food was great — but it was the most boring evening of my life. Frankie didn't crack a single joke, he wasn't funny, and he didn't bother with much conversation. Maybe it was a bad night — but at least Lena Horne was good.'

'After the way he had us all in hysterics every day on the set, it was more than a bit of a shock. Actually I vowed never to go out with him again, even if he asked me. He never did. And nor did I!'

In the smash-hit pantomime *Jack and the Beanstalk* at the Palladium, Frankie found a kindred spirit in his leading lady. Dora Bryan was the first actress ever to play the Dame in a pantomime at that illustrious establishment, and with Francis as Simple Simon the stage was set for a hilarious family outing.

Perhaps it was because Frankie was Pisces, Dora an Aquarian. Or that Dora was a devout Christian who believed implicitly in God, the Resurrection and Eternal Life. 'You can't argue about faith,' she would tell him. 'Either you've got it or you haven't.'

Either way, Frankie could argue about anything, and Dora proved the ideal sparring partner. And he loved nothing better than to get his teeth into a subject that had haunted him for as long as he could remember. Ever since, in fact, he first knelt by his bed as a little boy and prayed to Jesus to make him good and look after his mother, brother and sister.

'We had endless debates about spiritual things,' Dora recalls. 'We were so alike in many things — both of us perfectionists, both with quick tempers if something wasn't going right due to stupidity or negligence.'

The pantomime ran for a healthy eighteen weeks. Unfortunately for those who simply wanted nothing more than to enjoy themselves with a harmless night out in the West End, it was a time of heightened IRA activity.

Night after night an anonymous bomb warning would be phoned through to the box office — and invariably that meant the theatre had to be cleared. 'The IRA? Thick and sick!' was Frankie's terse comment, when he was cleared out of his dressing-room for the umpteenth time, and forced to stand around in the alley outside the stage door dressed as Simple Simon while the building was searched.

'It was all desperately boring,' Dora says, looking back on nights when all she could see of the audience was their backs surging towards the Exit doors. 'Sometimes the curtain would be rung down while I was in mid-leap in a dance. On average they were clearing the theatre three times a week, and seeing an audience stampeding for the doors in the middle of a performance is really quite demoralizing! I was particularly sorry for the groups of handicapped people.

'We put a brave face on it, but everybody was getting jolly fed up. We were supposed to file out of the stage door and hang around in our costumes in the street while they searched the theatre with sniffer dogs.

'After a couple of weeks of fun and games, Frankie had had enough. He said: "I'm not going out there any more. Come on into my dressing-room, and we'll raise a glass!" '

So Simple Simon and the Grand Dame sat with their feet up four floors above Argyll Street in Dressing-Room No. 1, sipping champagne and watching TV till the all-clear sounded.

9

Ups and Downs

The fickle finger of fate pointed all too frequently at Frankie Howerd, and did its worst. Charting his career on a graph reveals an alarming vista of peaks of euphoria and valleys of despond that would rival the Alps. In short, both in personality and the course his life took, Frankie was the original human yo-yo.

But how, when and why did it happen? How was it that a star of his calibre, idolized by millions, with a following that spanned all ages, could suddenly drop into the abyss of virtual anonymity?

Frankie's first fall from grace happened around 1957, and the seeds can be traced to his decision — which he later agreed was 'insane' — to turn down an offer by Bernard Delfont to star in another revue at the Prince of Wales called *Plaisirs de Paris*. Frankie had more grandiose aspirations. He wanted to be a 'comic actor' rather than a mere comic. Foolish Francis! He hadn't seen the amber warning lights thrown out by his screen efforts in *The Runaway Bus* (1954), *Jumping for Joy* (1955) or *A Touch of the Sun* (1956) which would have indicated to the most myopic observer that, though a brilliant clown in his own way, Frankie was no Chaplin.

Admittedly he had won plaudits with *Charley's Aunt* in 1956, with the *Times* critic giving him a friendly pat on the back by comparing him to an amiable carthorse — enough to turn anyone's head, ears and all. He persuaded himself that more fruitful pickings lay ahead. Delfont told him in no uncertain terms that he was making a big mistake, and hired Dickie Henderson instead. The show, predictably, was a safe bet for another long run, while Frankie found himself out in the sticks in the romantic farce *Hotel Paradiso*, performing to half-empty houses and tepid applause. They wanted their Francis to do a bit of ooh-ing and aah-ing, but the chaotic liaisons in the seedy hotel of the title would have none of it.

Frankie started to worry. He found it impossible to sleep, and would arrive at the theatre with his lids drooping and the bags under his eyes more pronounced than ever. 'Comedians are a pretty neurotic bunch,' he pointed out with his customary candour. 'When life's unkind the first thing that vanishes is your confidence – along with your salary. And that's fatal.'

Fatal? His self-confidence was close to being a terminal case, and the patient grew weaker still under a pressure Frankie could easily have lived without: a demand from Her Majesty's Inspectorate for *eight years* of back tax for unpaid monies. Rather than having the debt hanging over him, he paid up – and found precious little money left in the bank afterwards.

But Frankie Howerd and money were always uneasy bedfellows. He admitted, perhaps too often and too loudly, that he was 'hopeless' with it. Fortunately the people who were happy to help him earn it and invest it wisely were by and large worthy of his trust.

In his fifties heyday he once gave a fascinating insight into how much he earned and why, at the end of the day, he was left with only £20 a week from an income of £12,000 a year! Well, that's his story – but don't mock the afflicted. Poor Frankie never did have much of a head for figures.

'I like to live comfortably,' he said. 'But that doesn't mean I'm always wallowing in champagne or swanking at exclusive restaurants and nightclubs. I don't drink a lot, I don't smoke and I don't gamble.' So where did it all go?

'Start with my agent, who gets ten per cent. And my manager – there goes another ten per cent. Plus my pianist, chauffeur, dresser. They all have to be paid. My car is a Mercedes. I don't drive it myself, but I need it to get about in. Clothes – another big item.' Even for rumpled Frankie, who would fall asleep in a brand new suit, and wonder at the creases when he woke up? 'All right, I'm no Beau Brummel,' he admitted. 'But I have to look reasonably presentable. Though personally I'm happy to lounge around in almost anything. I reckon clothes cost me £15 a week. Plus £25 for stage suits, and I often get through three shirts in an evening . . .

'I entertain a lot. Although I'm virtually teetotal, I keep the bar at home stocked – and a supply of booze in my dressing-room. If I'm at the Palladium the kind of people who drop in there don't drink beer!

'Myself, I'm a steak and kidney type. But I can't just wander in off the street any more. I love my public, but there are times when they can get a bit too embarrassing. That means I have to go to places where they don't worry me — and those places are usually expensive.' Frankie always spoke his mind. 'I don't stay in theatrical digs any more. I'm expected to stay at the best hotel and that costs money. If you're top of the bill you can't leave a tanner under the plate.

'It doesn't stop there: if you're the star of the show you find plenty of people help you, and they're just as entitled to a tip as a waiter. I'm also charged for any seats I might want to give to important guests.

'And publicity: the cost of sending out two thousand photos every three months mounts up. Someone has to pay for the stamps. And for the secretary or publicity agent who sends them off. I also pay out £1,000 a year insurance, whether or not the theatre covers me.

'But after all that — I'm not complaining. I'm lucky to have anything left at all. And would Francis ever complain . . . ?' Perish the thought.

Frankie staggered everyone — not least himself — by joining the Old Vic production of *A Midsummer Night's Dream* to play Bottom the Weaver, and again the reviews were good, but the run, of necessity, was short. The salary hadn't been great, either.

Frankie had been a star for twelve years. But changes in technology and popular taste happened together, one feeding the other. Frankie, who always claimed he was a late starter in his personal life — not losing his virginity until his mid-twenties — was also a latecomer when it came to climbing into bed with television. As Ray Galton commented: 'Frankie felt that TV was a dangerous medium for him that could ruin his reputation if things went wrong.' Tony Hancock didn't have the same doubts and *Hancock's Half Hour* made the transition from radio to TV smoothly — and, as audience ratings were to prove, with staggering success.

A guest appearance on *What's My Line* had done nothing to alter his opinion. If anything, the disastrous Sunday night in March 1954 enhanced all Frankie's self-doubts. It was one of the top shows on TV, with Eamonn Andrews keeping order in the chair while the diverse personalities of Barbara Kelly, Isobel Barnett, David Nixon and Gilbert Harding tried to guess the job of the participants. Smiling David and grouchy Gilbert were the show's Mr Nice and Mr Nasty.

A phone call two days before brought chaos to the Howerd household. Harding was ill. Would Frankie take his place? The show went out live, and adlibbing, which was what it was all about, was never one of his strong points. But Frankie couldn't afford to turn down a chance to be seen by millions of viewers across the country.

Oh, Francis! Once he was in the hot seat at the BBC's Lime Grove Studios, with everyone around him bubbling with witty, elegant chatter, Frankie dried up completely. Even the odd stammer was worth a point! He would put on record afterwards that he felt 'like a rabbit trapped in a car's headlights, frozen with blind terror'. It was as bad as that. Sensing it, which wasn't too hard, Barbara Kelly even slipped him scraps of paper with questions hastily scrawled on them to put to the contender.

'We were always kind to strangers!' She still remembers the embarrassment. 'Frankie just lost his bottle completely from the moment he sat down. I felt particularly sorry for him because I'd had a similar experience only a month before.' Barbara had been flown to New York to make up the numbers on the US version of the same show, with the team headed by Steve Allen. 'The difference was that they tried to cold-shoulder me, ring the curtain down, not let me get a word in. I wasn't having any of that, I can tell you! We would never have been like that here. I took pity on poor Frankie and scribbled down questions for him. I don't think it helped very much, because he was too far gone!'

All in all, a bad night. The BBC switchboard was flooded with complaints, and next day the Press were merciless. Poor Francis, in cricketing parlance, retired hurt.

But at least when you're down you find out who your friends are. And Frankie found the value of true friendship and loyalty ran deeper than he could ever have imagined. Both those in the business and outside it rallied round. Writers offered to pen him scripts for nothing – he would have none of it, but he was greatly moved. Sunny Rogers quietly offered her life savings to his manager, Dennis Heymer, on the condition that Frankie didn't find out. Two weeks later a TV appearance came in that meant Dennis was able, gratefully, to decline.

Bernard Delfont was also on hand with the life belt during such 'dark times'. 'Frankie always had that great talent, he was an original. But unfortunately he also had his down-turns. He made mistakes — and paid for them dearly. I used to say that he made more come-backs than anyone else in show business.'

Delfont heard that Frankie was down, if not quite out. 'I felt sorry for him, and I put him into one of my summer shows — at Scarborough. He was very grateful. But as bad luck would have it, that summer was a heat wave from start to finish, and the show didn't do any business.'

David Lodge, a veteran of more than a hundred films, as well as numerous TV and radio appearances, was in the show. He arrived one morning to find Frankie on stage in a 900-seat theatre that was totally empty apart from three bemused figures in the front row — the carpenter and two electricians. They had been hauled from their work backstage and summarily dispatched to Row 1 to watch the star go through his entire act — just for them.

'Of course they were laughing,' recalls Lodge. 'But it was rather spooky in that near-empty theatre. Frankie did the whole act word for word, with all the "ooohs" and "aaahs", every pause and syllable in its rightful place. Every innuendo and nuance was planned. Not a single adlib. I joined them and brought the audience up to four! Oh, make that five: there was a mouse scuttling around on the stage behind him, too . . .'

As Frankie put it in a card home to Lee Young: 'Blazing sunshine day after day. That's all we need!' He was getting £250 a week, but the sight of rows of empty seats gaping at him every night bankrupted his spirits. With every passing day his depression grew.

'He was disappointed. So was I,' says Delfont. 'But I was grateful that I had at least repaid him in some small way for the financial gains he had made me — as well as himself, of course!' What he meant was: count the noughts! Frankie at his top-earning capacity was bringing them in by the coach-load, when he would

get his four-figure salary – plus a slice of the cake – and deserve
every penny of it.

Frankie had another faithful ally, man's best friend, his boxer
dog Red. In the quiet nights when he took himself off for lonely
strolls to walk his pet around the streets of Notting Hill, Frankie
would weep silent tears – not of self-pity, but for the depth of
the affection that so many people had for him.

In April 1957 the overwhelming sense of failure drove him into
a Harrow, Middlesex, nursing-home suffering from nervous
exhaustion. 'What they meant is that I was on the verge of a
nervous breakdown,' he told Simon Ward of the *Daily Sketch*.
In the days he was inside he had time to take stock of himself.
'Ambition, that's what caused it. I've been a star for years now,
but deep down I'm as nervy and insecure as ever.'

There had been another *Follies*-type spectacular in the pipeline,
but he had had to withdraw from it, and reckoned it cost him
£20,000. 'How I envy the placid types who never want more than
they've got!' he said, with a sudden burst of rancour.

At least Red was there to welcome him on his return home,
along with his feed and friend Lee Young. In those days Frankie
was living in a small apartment in Holland Park, with Lee in the
flat below. The rest in the nursing-home had done him good and
for a time he managed a more rational view on life's hardships.

'It taught me not to be broken-hearted over failure. I had
so many other things that were worthwhile: mainly people. The
friends who had been so kind. And I had a nice flat, good
furniture, pictures on the walls. And my dog. I was lucky,
really.'

Red was a great slobbery gambolling brute with a sense of
humour as peculiar as his master's and a timing all his own.
Frankie loved him, and wouldn't hear a word said against him.
He took Red round the country when he toured in variety, and
stage managers throughout Britain sighed and reached for the
towel, ready to mop up – or throw it in.

Lew Lane remembers the trick he used to play when he went
backstage to make sure his star was in good fettle. 'Frankie would
be sitting in front of the mirror, and Red would be in a corner
gnawing a bone. I would make a mock rush at his master with

loud threatening noises, and Red would spring to his defence. The only trouble was that he always sprang on Frankie's back! I've seen them topple over on to the floor in a heap with Frankie shouting and cursing: "*Gerroff me! Do you hear – gerroff!*" It never failed.

Once Lew was with Sunny Rogers accompanying Frankie on an advance trip to Birmingham to check the scenery and props for the pantomime *Jack and the Beanstalk*. As usual Red was trotting along at their heels. By now he was getting on – 'His coat was all mottled, and there were nasty lumps all over his back,' Lew recalls. 'We walked on to the set of the forest glade – and, you've guessed it! Red made a beeline for the nearest tree and cocked his leg on it! The stage manager was livid. Frankie just shrugged it off.'

Alfred Marks and his wife Paddy remember a close encounter with the 'Hound of the Basket-case' when they attended one of Frankie's parties in Holland Park. 'This boxer was enormous, a real slobber-chops, which he adored. It looked extremely dangerous, but in fact it was very friendly. Margaret Rutherford was sitting on a low stool eating chicken off a plate, chatting to us. She turned away to talk to someone and next thing – *whoof*! The food had gone. And Red was chewing away contentedly, quite unabashed.

'Margaret looked astounded, and complained loudly to the host. But Frankie only said: "Oh . . . Don't stop him dear, he's enjoying it!" That dog always did get priority to the guests.'

Character actor Alfred Molino was a regular in the early Frankie Howerd TV shows. On one series in the early sixties he found himself embroiled in various misadventures, playing anything from a temperamental film director to a vicar.

They were at the BBC's Lime Grove studios. One Monday morning Frankie rushed up to him and said excitedly: 'Come and have lunch with me. I've just heard that Ginger Rogers has started rehearsing.'

It transpired that the Hollywood legend had been brought over to star in a musical, live on TV, called *Charisma*. Frankie, unashamedly smitten, dragged Molino over to the General Smuts pub nearby which had a large upstairs room used by the BBC for rehearsals. They took their seats at a table facing the doors, and ordered cheese sandwiches while they waited for the great movie star to appear.

There was one other lunchtime companion that day. Red, the boxer.

Alfred relates the dire events that happened next. 'Frankie was all keyed up, positively trembling with anticipation. He was like a star-struck kid. But he had this terrible boxer dog with him, which by that time had grown very old and was covered with lumps and bumps, poor thing.

'Eventually the doors opened, and out swept Ginger Rogers looking absolutely fabulous in a white dress. And before Frankie could stop him, this wretched mangy beast leaped out from under the table and pelted across the room and jumped up at her, putting its paws on her dress and slobbering all over her. There were paw marks everywhere. The lady was not at all pleased. In fact, she was hopping mad. Frankie was completely mortified, trying to stutter his apologies while bellowing at the dog: "Red, come here! Get off her!" '

There were bits and pieces of work coming Frankie's way, but the tide of popularity had receded into the hazy distance and showed little sign of being on the turn.

Frankie decided to take a holiday with his business manager Dennis Heymer, figuring that things couldn't get much worse. But they could. Very much worse.

Dennis drove them in Frankie's Mercedes to a remote corner of Wales in the foothills of the Brecon Beacons. There they found a small hotel by the River Usk where they could relax, far from the worldly problems that were giving Frankie a daily migraine. Frankie had always loved the countryside. He had bought a small cottage in Reigate, Surrey, but would eventually sell up and find his own corner of paradise in Somerset.

For now, he decided to try his hand at horse riding. He described the results to columnist Jack Bentley of the *Sunday Mirror* − once the hospital had patched him up. 'We were high up in the mountains, and I'd fallen off a couple of times. But nothing serious. I was negotiating a narrow path along a clifftop, when suddenly the beast bolted. I heaved on the reins, shouting and yelling for it to stop − but the reins snapped, and the thing

shot off down the steep slope with me still clinging to it. I couldn't
hang on — and off I came. Somehow the horse rolled on top of
me, and one of its hooves caught me in the head.'

Ouch! Dennis galloped off like the cavalry for help. Frankie
suffered a broken wrist, concussion and severe multiple bruising.
His ribs ached for a month. He would be under treatment from
a nerve specialist for the next three years, prompting his
scriptwriter friend Ray Galton to try to raise a smile by
commenting: 'Frank, there can't be a bloody door down the whole
of Harley Street that you haven't gone through.'

Frankie, the confirmed hypochondriac, nodded lugubriously.
'You're right,' he rejoined. 'And that includes Wimpole Street
and all the rest, too.'

But it was the start of a period of bleak depression, with little
work, less money, and no prospects. Frankie even nursed thoughts
of running a pub, but his friends managed to dissuade him of
that notion. Fate's fickle finger was giving him a rough time.

To an outsider, he still appeared comfortably off, with no sign
of his haemorrhaging funds, almost all of which had ended up
in the hungry maw of the tax man. His top floor flat was rented
from Ben Warriss, who owned the converted Victorian villa. It
was comfortable; a trifle opulent with embossed maroon Regency
wallpaper, but without being overly luxurious.

A lot of the furniture was Frankie's favoured antique, and the
bookshelves contained anything from Agatha Christie thrillers and
a biography of Madame Pompadour to the full set of the
Encyclopedia Britannica. A baby grand piano sat next to a pile
of classical records, predominantly Beethoven. For a public
vulgarian, Frankie had a remarkably cultural range of interests
— just another clue to the complexity of his nature. But then,
he did have an IQ of 163.

No one stood by him more loyally than another friend, Ernie
Wise.

Little Ern first met Frankie in 1961, shortly after a TV show
Morecambe and Wise made called *Running Wild* had been aired
— and flopped. 'We were all of us struggling. Frankie was going
through a tough time, and our series had gone up the spout.
We were at a charity function, and I remember on that first

meeting commiserating with him, and trying to cheer him up.'

Ernie describes himself as 'always a great jollier-up of comics who are going through bad patches. I've been through it myself, so I know!' They discussed failure – Frankie, as usual, analysing everything into the ground, and Ernie telling him: 'Funny thing, however great your success, you never get rid of the taste of failure. You wear the scars for ever.' Frankie could only nod in agreement.

At least Morecambe and Wise had each other to lean on in the crisis moments. 'Frankie had a much tougher time than we did,' says Ernie. 'We had one another for support. He really had no one, even though his friends stood by him and did all they could. But it's tough when you're a single act and the phone doesn't ring.'

Frankie was always grateful for the advice and sympathy, and Ernie and Doreen Wise were high on the guest list at his parties. They would also see a lot of the comic when they took a holiday in Malta, and found themselves at dinner parties in Frankie's house – named The Forum – on the clifftop near Valetta.

Ernie learned to watch for the warning signs if Frankie was feeling petulant. It meant trouble ahead. 'He was always very good to us, and a most generous host. But if someone in the group said something that annoyed him or he felt had stepped out of line, he would turn on them – and he had a very sharp tongue. Usually it was heavy sarcasm. He could be very prickly. Luckily he was a Morecambe and Wise fan, and we never fell out!'

Back home Ernie would invite Frankie to the White City dog track when his own greyhound was running. 'It was called Short Fat Hairy Legs – and it never won a bean!' But they had some good nights out, even if they never went home rich.

Frankie loathed making after-dinner speeches. Even opening a summer fair was a fête worse than death. But when the Water Rats – the famous entertainers' charity – laid on a tribute to Morecambe and Wise, and Lew Lane asked him if he would at least consider saying a few words, Frankie agreed on the spot. Provided he could be part of a gag they'd planned in advance.

The event was the prestigious Personality of the Year Award, a major highlight, with a celebrity audience gathered in the Lancaster Room of the Savoy for the occasion. Frankie made his speech from the top table, the plaudits flowing thick and fast on Ernie's unbowed head — while Eric, totally ignored and unmentioned, sat with a 'What about me?' expression on his bespectacled features.

Frankie heaped praises on Ernie for 'all those marvellous scripts you've written', and conjuror David Nixon, as King Rat, presented the 'one with the short fat hairy legs' — not the greyhound — with the prized silver trophy. They took it to the edge before Eric was finally allowed to join in the fun and be part of the act, too.

Of all the people on the inside track who watched Frankie's spectacular fall into the abyss and long, agonizing crawl back into public acclaim, none was closer to him than Lew Lane. A big man like Frankie, with a large and generous personality, Lew is a former stand-up comedian who first felt the clarion call to stardom when he won a talent contest at the Empire, Dudley, as a twelve-year-old boy ventriloquist, along with his dummy Johnny Brown. Lew had made similar tracks to Frankie on the arduous, frequently heart-breaking slog through countless small theatres and clubs, where the customers prefer to drink than listen. But Lew turned promoter, and by the fifties was the acknowledged king of the clubs when it came to booking acts, from unknown snake charmers to Bob Hope, Sammy Davis Junior and Frank Sinatra.

It was Lew Lane who was responsible for the extraordinary shift in the ebb and flow of Frankie's fortunes — and who would carry him on a high tide to the top again. He had heard Frankie describe his breakdown. 'Life became a long dark tunnel and I thought I would never emerge from it.' He knew a decade of heady success had ended almost as abruptly as it began. Lew had first-hand experience of the way television was entrenching itself as the bastion of entertainment, crushing the live variety halls and plundering radio audiences.

In the good years Lew saw the generous side of Frankie. 'When he had money and was earning well, he was generous to a fault. He had a passion for old films and we used to go almost every month to search out an old movie that was playing somewhere in London. He seemed to think that because he was the star he had to pay for both our seats. We used to have quite noisy arguments. Of course I did the driving, so at least I paid for the petrol.'

In London they would go to Shepherd's Bush or Notting Hill Gate. If Frankie was touring they would often find an old movie in the local fleapit – this was before the modern multiplexes were even a twinkle in an architect's eye.

Frankie's favourite film was *Kiss of Death*, a black-and-white 1947 thriller about a psychopathic killer sent to rub out a squealer. It starred Victor Mature, Brian Donlevy and Karl Malden, but was most notable for being the film where Richard Widmark, giggling crazily, pushed an old lady in a wheelchair down a flight of stairs to her death.

'We first saw it in Birmingham, in some side street cinema,' recalled Lew. 'Frankie enjoyed it so much he made me go back and see it again for the next two days running. And he kept imitating Widmark's giggle! He'd suddenly shriek it out for no reason, and it was chillingly realistic. I had to keep telling him to stop it, or he'd get himself locked up!'

It was Richard Widmark's first film, and it won him an Oscar nomination. Alas, Frankie never got to be that lucky.

Lew booked him into more theatres and clubs than he could remember. They were crying out for him, and he duly obliged, remembering Ernie Wise's stricture that clubs were 'a licence to print money'. Big clubs only now, like the Diamond Horseshoe, Manchester, and the Castaways and the Big Night Out in Birmingham for Delfont. And summer seasons wherever there was a good sea breeze blowing.

The clubs in London were smaller, more intimate. They had names like the Masquerade and the Gargoyle, the 50 Club in Frith Street and the Mandrake that was frequented by jazz musicians. Some of them were run by gangsters like the Krays, but Frankie never became enmeshed in that kind of dangerous web. In the sixties Lew was responsible for the shows in two of the top Mayfair clubs, Churchills and the 21, where the clientele was mainly comprised of swarthy-looking gentlemen of Middle Eastern appearance sprinkling notes of a high denomination around like so much confetti.

To help Frankie end his run of bad luck and drag his old pal out of the doldrums, Lew had a word in the right places and got him a month at the Blue Angel, a haunt of the rich, the famous and possibly the unsavoury too. It was one of the in-places, starting late, ending as the nightingales stopped singing and the dawn came up over Berkeley Square.

The Blue Angel attracted top acts like the milky-voiced crooner Hutch, and Lew figured it was ideal for Frankie. A small dance floor, packed tables, intimate lighting. The walls in the bar were actually draped with fishing nets, but whether that was to make the hookers or the hooked feel at home no one ever revealed. Cabaret started at 11.00 p.m., sometimes later. It could go on until 2.00 a.m.

Frankie was paid £60 a week. Privately he confided to Lew that he would have done it for half the money.

Midway through the Blue Angel run, Edith Howard died. Frankie was devastated – but like the true trouper he was, he went on at midnight and somehow got through his act. 'I had lost someone I loved deeply. I felt totally empty, drained of all feeling and all sense of reality,' he would say of those dreadful hours. Frankie and his mother had been close all his life, almost obsessively so, and he never forgot the encouragement she gave him when he had needed it most.

But something else cut him to the quick on that sunless June day. 'I went to the post office up the road to post some letters to friends telling them what had happened. A man I passed in the street called out: "Cheer up, Frankie!"

'I was at one of the lowest points of my life, feeling quite awful – and here was this man expecting me to go around with a great big grin on my face. What do they do with people who go round grinning all the time? I'll tell you. They send two men in white coats to lock them up . . .'

No use telling Frankie about the price of fame. He was inconsolable for days, and his sister Betty came to stay with him and help him through the dark hours ahead.

It was at Churchill's club that Frankie witnessed the start of an incident that has gone down in the annals of Fleet Street. The comic popped in for a drink to while away an hour before strolling

along to the Blue Angel in Berkeley Square where he was due to
go on at midnight.

He was spotted in a quiet corner by two show business writers
from the tabloids − we'll call them David and Walter − who
were 'doing the rounds' of the clubs, sniffing out stories. In those
days they were known as the Rat Pack, later to be down-graded
to the Mouse Pack as the quality of this literary paparazzi
degenerated. But in those days Fleet Street was fun, and full of
mischief rather than mischief-makers.

The pair sat with Frankie to watch the cabaret, jotting down
notes over a bottle of champagne. Frankie, who enjoyed the
company of professionals, was happy to welcome them, and
maybe get his name in the papers too. The show ended with a
spectacular display from the chorus as the line of beauties, arms
linked, came high-kicking out in pitch darkness glowing with
luminous make-up.

Frankie had to leave − just as two of the girls came over to
sit with the lads from the Street of Sin and Ink. A couple of hours
and a similar number of bottles of bubbly later, the pair had
persuaded the girls − who conveniently shared a flat in Bayswater
− to take them back for a nightcap.

It was 5.00 a.m. and still dark before Walter got home in the
cold hour before dawn, and tiptoed up the stairs to the bedroom.
Not wishing to wake his wife and have to answer awkward
questions, he undressed in the bathroom and edged into the room,
heading towards the bed.

Maybe it was the effects of the champagne, or his efforts of
the previous hours, but in the total blackness he banged into the
dressing-table . . . and his wife sat up abruptly. And screamed.
'Walter! You're all aglow!'

And he was, like an apparition from outer space, glowing from
head to foot with luminous body make-up.

Walter said ruefully after the divorce went through: 'My mind
went blank. What can you say? The only excuse I might have used
is that I met this alien in the garden . . . but it probably wouldn't
have washed.'

When they told Frankie about it, his eyebrows shot up. 'But
I bet you wish *you* had!' he said.

*

It all happened so fast that Francis hardly had time to draw breath before he realized he was back on top again.

A regular annual chore which he was always pleased to fulfil was the annual *Evening Standard* theatre awards ceremony at the Savoy, as personal guest of the *Daily Express* chief Sir Max Aitken. It was the one occasion when Frankie enjoyed clambering to his feet and bumbling through the speech they insisted that he make — even if, looking around at the winners and losers, his stock line was 'The best actors here tonight are the ones who don't get it!' How true — and the star-studded audience appreciated it more than anyone.

Part of that audience in the 1962 event was Peter Cook, the tall and languid half of the anarchic Cook–Dudley Moore duo, who was there to pick up the award for the best musical *Beyond the Fringe* with his three cohorts: diminutive Dud, Jonathan Miller and Alan Bennett. Nurtured in the restless hothouse of the Cambridge Footlights, their satirical style of humour was winning an army of fans. They were in the process of opening a new club in Soho called the Establishment, a name deliberately chosen as the very antithesis of what it stood for. Its nightly fare would include the outrageous likes of Lenny Henry.

Cook and Co. found Frankie's irreverent speech just the kind of thing that might appeal to their new, irreverent membership. Frankie took over — at £400 a week. The upstairs club a few yards off Old Compton Street was packed solid. The people were the trendy set, college students, graduates, the intelligentsia of the future. The sight of Frankie's untidy, reluctant figure wandering out into the smoke-hazy room to address them *confidentially, you understand* somehow reduced them to instant laughter.

They roared at his opening. 'Satire? I'll tell you what satire is. 'Ow's this then? "*Piss off!*" ' He went on to inquire why a sausage should be funnier than a lamb chop, and spent lengthy minutes in deep analysis over such a vital question.

Whatever chord Frankie had touched, no one could rightly explain. But it resonated into the chic confines of Chelsea, Belgravia and beyond, and the word went round on the grapevine: there was somebody rather special at the Establishment. Someone who shouldn't be missed.

The word reached the ear of Ned Sherrin, who was busy putting together a brand-new idea for television that would reflect the rebellious cult of the sixties. 'TW3' was how it came to be known, or *That Was the Week That Was*, fronted by David Frost, with its brassy opening theme sung by Millicent Martin, and a crowd of young eager-beaver humorists, headed by the manic brilliance of John Cleese, doing their darndest to rock the real Establishment to its smug foundations.

Ned Sherrin, one of the wittiest and most enduring of broadcasters, took a look at Frankie Howerd propping up his stool on the tiny stage in Soho. In all he came three times. He liked what he saw, and he took a gamble. He invited Frankie to join the TW3 crowd.

'I didn't see it as a gamble, even if other people did,' says Sherrin, recalling those heady days. 'I had known Francis for years – he was always lumbering up to me at parties! And out of all the comics around, he was my favourite clown. I thought he would be perfect for TW3 – he elevated satire to the level of the kitchen sink!'

Frankie Howerd's first comeback was complete with a night of triumph on Saturday, 6 April 1963. Afterwards he would say casually that he only agreed to go on it because it was David Frost's birthday.

The viewing millions of what had unkindly but accurately been dubbed the 'Snob and Satire Show' saw Francis wander out, prop himself on a stool, stare mournfully into the camera – and talk. His target was the Budget, and in particular the unfortunate Chancellor of the Exchequer, Reginald Maudling.

'*And I put it to you, ladies and gentle-men, I put it to you . . . and you can put it where you like, madam . . . !*' Next day the whole country was doing the talking, and laughing, about the rambling monologue that lasted thirteen hilarious minutes and seemed to be mostly adlib. In fact Frankie, who was nobody's April Fool, started working out the act two days previously with Johnny Speight, down to the last stutter and splutter.

'I spent most of the day rehearsing in front of a mirror – even to putting my tongue out,' he said.

When he was getting made up, Frost popped a head round the door. 'You don't need make-up,' he said reassuringly. 'You need a miracle.'

The miracle happened half an hour later. The cameramen were laughing so much they almost missed their marks, and in the control room the producer and his staff were in fits. Next day the phone started ringing in his flat, the Press crowded his doorstep, and Frankie Howerd knew the welcome mat had been put out for him once more.

That night Frankie rang Lew Lane at home in Muswell Hill, North London. His voice was choked. 'You know, Lew, it *was* like a miracle when people started laughing at me again,' he said.

10
. . . And The Other Men

Sorry, Missus, but Frankie Howerd was not just camp. He was most unashamedly, outrageously gay. His sexual proclivities were a byword in the business, though surprisingly few revelations of them ever crept out into the public domain. Quite shameless was our Francis.

The truth is that after some genuine romantic dallyings with the opposite sex in his younger days, the women in his life were largely a cosmetic exercise. From his thirties Frankie had allowed the other side of his nature to hold sway, and the women he felt most at home with were elderly actresses like the two Hermiones (Baddeley and Gingold) who would be regular guests in his 'inner sanctum' of parties for his personal friends, along with ladies of mature vintage like Binnie Hale, Zsa Zsa Gabor and Margaret Rutherford.

Frankie loved them all dearly – in his way. And in turn they loved him back, displaying a touching and universal loyalty to him.

'Frankie did everything he could to keep the fact that he was gay from being made general knowledge,' says Jeanne Mockford. 'The public never really knew. To them he was just camp.

'It was always a cover-up that he would take June Whitfield or Betty or myself to a function. He would usually take somebody of the opposite sex. He was very discreet and never careless. I much preferred that. I don't want people broadcasting their sexual preferences for all and sundry to know about – I find that objectionable. Sex is a private thing. People in the business knew. But to the outside world, Frankie was just camp, and fun. And that's the way it should be. And does it matter anyway?'

At the 1966 Variety Club luncheon in his honour, the River Room at the Savoy Hotel was packed to the rafters with celebrities, media folk and personalities from all walks of show business. In the VIP bar beforehand over pre-lunch aperitifs, someone remarked: 'One thing about Frankie, he can certainly put bums on seats.'

Tommy Cooper, passing by, overheard. 'Safest place for them!' he said laconically, and stalked on into the dining-room.

But Frankie had his own methods of propositioning his targets, without any compunction or embarrassment. He was quite bare-faced, if not bare-cheeked, about it. Sometimes he would pounce with scarcely an introduction.

Costume designer Joan Ellacott recalls an incident in the filming of *Jumping for Joy* at the White City dog track. The artists' caravans were moored in the car park, and Frankie's lecherous eye fell on a young handsome dresser, whose first film it was. He beckoned him into his trailer. 'What's your name?' he asked.

'Tom,' said Tom.

'Right, Tom — bend over!' said Frankie without more ado.

Tom fled, pale-faced, and ran up to Joan. 'I'm not going back in there!' he said. 'Is that what they mean by the casting-couch?'

The legendary American comic Jack Benny, who shared a dressing-room with Frankie on the star-studded Royal Variety bill in 1950, was heard to remark afterwards: 'I thought you had only one Queen of England!'

Frankie was careful not to upset those who employed him. *Carry On* producer Peter Rogers and director Gerald Thomas had heard all the gossip. So had BBC Light Entertainment Head Bobby Jaye. None of them saw any evidence of it. Nor did Lord Delfont, who hosted the actual Queen on numerous Royal Variety shows. 'Frankie never made a pass at me. I think he was too much in awe of me to try anything like that!' says the veteran impresario. 'I never had any idea of what his private life was like. He kept that to himself. As far as I was concerned, it was his own affair.'

Kevin Francis, a producer in the fast lane of films and television, could have been useful to Frankie's career when it was in one of its recurring slumps. In 1990 he met the comic in the famous bar at Pinewood Studios. 'Over a glass of sherbert I talked to him about a game show I was putting together,' Kevin recalls. 'It would have been a marvellous vehicle for him. Like Wogan on *Blankety Blank*, which was supposed to be a quiz show but in fact was all about Wogan being silly with the guests, it would have been built around him.'

Frankie went for it in a big way. 'He was on the phone with fresh ideas every week and worked solidly on it from his home

for three months. He would come out to discuss it with me. The
first time we met, he said: "If you want to negotiate, let's lock
the door and do it on our own!" He was quite outrageously
obvious.' But Kevin refused to take it seriously, and the phrase
became an in-joke between them.

Then out of the blue the phone rang, and Frankie was saying:
'It's a wonderful show, but now I'm going to do you the greatest
favour of your life. I'm sorry, but I can't do it. I've realized that
I'm wrong for it . . .'

'I was dumbfounded,' says Kevin, a man not normally short
of words. 'But it showed me just how professional he was,
suddenly to stop working and chuck it all in after giving so much
to it.'

The man who shared Frankie's home and his life in the early years
was Lee Young, feed, friend and fall-guy for Frankie's shafts of
wit. Lee's real name was Jimmy, but because of a certain other
entertainer who was doing rather well at the time with songs like
'Too Young', he decided to change it.

When Frankie heard about it, he was horrified. 'Lee?' he cried.
'You can't call yourself *Lee*! It makes you sound like a
Chinaman.'

Lee said stubbornly: 'Well, it's my middle name, and I'm
keeping it. At least no one else will have it.'

'Please yourself!' said Frankie. And Lee it became.

In the seventies Frankie flew to Australia to make a film called
Up the Convicts, a sort of 'Down Under Pompeii'. Lee went with
him − and ended up staying. He found an apartment in Elizabeth
Bay, on the fringe of the notorious King's Cross area. But he made
the long flight back for Frankie's funeral to pay his last respects
to his old friend.

Lee became a public relations consultant for cruise line
entertainers plying the South Pacific, as well as forming his own
show for 'Returned ex-Servicemen's Clubs' in Oz. He also did
a spot of stand-up comedy.

He met Frankie in the early fifties when he was helping out with
the Crazy Gang, and happily accepted an invitation to become
his stooge on *Frankie Howerd Goes East* and *Fine Goings On*.
His lasting memory: 'We were out in Cairo. Poor Frankie kept

getting gippy (as in Egypt) tummy, and Eric Sykes had to take his place. What a trip!'

Lee remembers his friend hitting the roof after a bad press. 'He became very angry and ropable.' Ropable? 'It's an Aussie term for losing your temper – string 'em up! He took everything personally. He would yell and scream – but you knew where you were with him, unlike Benny Hill who always bottled things up. And he was a wonderful friend in a crisis. But he was terrible about remembering things like people's birthdays!'

Frankie did take the occasional risk at outraging authority. The BBC's Richard Willcox is one who had an eye-opening experience of his wayward tendencies. As a senior producer he first met the comic in the Mayfair headquarters of entrepreneur Robert Stigwood, where Frankie enjoyed open house and access to his bar in the plush suite near Hyde Park.

Frankie's agent Tessa Le Bars had an office in the Stigwood emporium at No. 67, Brook Street, and he would use it to meet his writers and have lengthy script discussions that went on far into the night. The bar was always open and Frankie would dispense largesse with the generosity of a host whose horizons knew no bounds.

Richard had gone there to discuss the new *Frankie Howerd Variety Show* – and it was one meeting he would never forget in a hurry. 'He propositioned me within minutes of our shaking hands and sitting down to talk about the show. It was going to be quite spectacular for radio, live from the Adelphi Theatre, one of the biggest series the BBC had ever done.'

Frankie shook his hand. Willcox accepted a Scotch. Without further ado Frankie grimaced and said: 'I've got this bad back' – he pointed a hand up between his shoulder blades. 'Do you think you could rub some ointment into it?' – He gestured at a tube of Vaseline on the table.

Ointment? Vaseline? Willcox stared, nonplussed. 'Well, Frankie – I – er – ' Now he found himself doing the stuttering.

Frankie peeled off his shirt. 'Yes, right here . . .'

Willcox stammered: 'But, er – '

'Are you married?' the comic asked. And now he was unbuttoning his trousers.

'Yes,' said Willcox, striving to retain his composure. 'I'm a happily married man. Since you ask. Very happily married – ' The trousers descended to the floor.

The producer eyed his star standing in front of him with his trousers round his ankles, and was beset by momentary doubts about the future of the programme he had come to discuss.

After the proverbial pregnant pause, he finally managed to say: 'I've heard about you, Frankie. I'm sorry. It's not on.'

Frankie reluctantly reached down and hoisted his trousers up. 'Please yourself,' he said. 'But if you haven't tried it, you don't know what you're missing!'

'And from that moment on, neither of us ever mentioned it again,' says Willcox, safely ensconced in his first-floor office in the Light Entertainment headquarters off Langham Place. 'But for all that, I couldn't help liking the silly sod!'

When word got round, someone groaned and said: 'Oh God! Whenever Frankie's on the show we're going to be known as the British Bendover Corporation . . .'

In the Adelphi show, a young, handsome photographer turned up to take pictures during rehearsals. Willcox remembers it vividly: 'Frankie took one look at him – and they both disappeared for an hour and a half. They came back later, with Frankie looking more rumpled than ever, but with a smile on his face that lasted the rest of the day.'

If he took a shine to you, Frankie would come out with it straight away. So to speak. But once he had been rebuffed, he never pursued it. The object of his potential devotion would often become a good showbiz chum, as if nothing of a devious – or deviant – nature had ever been suggested. Frankie simply forgot all about it.

The critic and broadcaster Alan Frank, who once worked as a film extra, was a face in the crowd in the 1956 comedy *A Touch of the Sun*, when he had first-hand experience – well, almost – of Frankie's tendencies. The star approached him as he was having a cup of tea during the afternoon break by the caterer's tent. 'How about it?' said Francis, without preamble. 'Like to come to my caravan?'

Alan, fortunately blessed with a rapier wit which he could unsheath in a tight corner, responded: 'Sorry, Frankie. It's my day off.'

Frankie gave him a lopsided grin. 'It's your loss,' was all he said. And on several films after that they met and chatted as if it had never happened. Which, come to think of it, it hadn't.

Barry Cryer, the white-haired but ever-youthful doyen of radio comedy writing, spent many hours with Frankie mulling over scripts. Only once did he get the direct approach. 'Frankie produced a bottle of embrocation, and asked me to rub his back,' Barry says. 'I told him: "*Not the old massage ploy, Frank!*"' And he never bothered again. He took his rebuffs well — and there were plenty of them. But he would try it on with anybody and everybody.'

Fellow scriptwriter Ray Galton shrugs in wry relief. 'Frankie never chased me — and I didn't know whether to be flattered or not! But he loved to quiz me on my sex life, just as he did with a lot of people, often perfect strangers at a first meeting. It could be a cocktail party, or a dinner. He was a very social animal.

'But he fancied himself as a psychoanalyst, and he would launch into the most intense cross-examinations that would absolutely stun his victim. He had a very dominant physical presence, too. You were immediately aware of him the moment he walked into a room, and he was not one to be a shrinking violet.' In fact, Galton concedes: 'I can't think of anyone I ever met who was more dominating. If he didn't know you, Frankie would size you up for a few minutes — then go straight in. Asking intimate questions about your sexual preferences — it was weird. But I don't think it was prurience, Frankie just wanted to embarrass people and see how they reacted. He was fascinated with human behaviour.'

Lew Lane, who had heard all the stories, was slightly disconcerted at their first meeting. He knocked on the door of his star's dressing-room, to be greeted by a genial roar of 'Come in, I'm not going to rape you!'

'Glad to hear it,' Lew muttered to himself, edging in.

After that it became a regular greeting.

Lew became a trusted friend, often dropping by for a script discussion or a social drink at Frankie's home. He became used to Frankie suddenly breaking off their chat to reach for the phone and call up a nearby massage parlour. Fifteen minutes later the doorbell would ring, and a young masseur with good looks and an eager-to-please smile would be on the doorstep.

With a brief: 'Back in a minute', Frankie would retreat into the bedroom and close the door, leaving Lew to study the paper or stare into space while he enjoyed an hour's massage. 'Whatever this entailed, who knows?' Lew remarked. 'But he was noticeably more relaxed and in a better humour afterwards. It obviously did him good.'

Some of those who knew him intimately have advanced the startling theory that as a small boy Frankie was sexually abused by his father on Sergeant Howard's intermittent visits home. One, who would engage in lengthy debates with him about life and love, is certain of it. 'This would explain so much about Frank's secrecy,' she says. 'About his attitudes, his basic dislike for Authority, the ultimate father figure. About his sexual problems, his aggression, his complexities – and his self-doubts and guilt.'

Guilt? 'You could sense it in many subtle ways. His constant analysis of your sex life was not just uncomfortable, it was positively unhealthy. He had this enormous, overpowering love for his mother – but when it came to talking about his father it was as if there was a mental block. He just wouldn't say anything. It was so strange, like forbidden territory.'

Asked the inevitable question, at the height of his sixties' fame, 'Why have you never been married?' Frankie would usually brush it aside with a short laugh and a disarming quip. But when cornered by a particularly persistent interviewer he took refuge in the 'Lonely Man' gambit.

'I've been tempted many times and succumbed to temptation many times,' he said. 'But fundamentally I'm a very shy person, and I've always been shy with women.'

Interviewer (craftily): 'So naturally you prefer men's company?'

Frankie (honest and open): 'One doesn't just choose to be a bachelor. Twice I was going to get engaged, but both times ended unhappily – in sickness and death. Because one ship has passed, you don't necessarily have to grab another because you feel the need to sail the sea.'

The interviewer, understandably frustrated, could only sail as close to the wind as he dared in those days by bitchily ending his last paragraph with the words: 'His handsome young manager beckoned to him from a waiting car . . .'

11

Carry On

Frankie Howerd broke into films doing the one thing he was never able to do in real life – drive. After crashing through the hedgerows of the West Country and embedding his Army lorry in a tree, you would expect him to be a trifle apprehensive about taking the wheel of a coach. Especially when the title was *The Runaway Bus*. Not Francis. He played Percy Lamb, the hapless driver of a BOAC coach trying to get his passengers to London Airport through a pea-souper fog. On board are an assortment of characters including a police officer, a glamorous air hostess, a mild gardening enthusiast, a flighty blonde and a militant reformist for the League of Positive Thought, in the redoubtable shape of Margaret Rutherford. Two of the party are bullion thieves, and there's a fortune in gold in the boot – along with a bound and gagged body.

The story, as one critic would remark on its release, was 'tailor-made' for Frankie. What he didn't know was that it was just that – a vehicle in every sense for his spluttering indignation, specially written for him by director Val Guest.

It all came about through a chance meeting with columnist Peter Noble, a veteran of the show business scene and himself a former actor, who had interviewed him on several occasions.

Frankie cornered him at a reception at the Café Royal, and without preamble demanded: ' 'Ere, why can't you get me into films? You know everybody in the film world. How about it?'

It was true. If anybody knew everybody, that person was Peter Noble. The columnist raised a restraining hand against the sudden onslaught. 'OK Frankie, I'll try. Leave it with me.'

Peter arranged a meeting with another old friend, the director Val Guest, who lived down the road in St John's Wood, close enough to Lord's cricket ground to cop a broken window with a six from the pitch. Frankie said: 'I've got this funny idea about playing a bus driver who loses his bus – '

'Say no more!' said Guest. The director scuttled off to a shelf where dozens of scripts, semi-scripts, treatments and single-page ideas were stacked. As Peter Noble would remark: 'That man has a complete library of ideas stored in his house. He's quite incredible. All you need is to turn the key — and he'll have it ready.'

Or almost ready. Frankie had unlocked an idea that had been gathering dust on the shelf. Val Guest came back with it, and for the next hour the three of them pored over the plot. It thickened with the fog as they discussed it. Finally Frankie asked: 'What do I do now?'

Guest replied: 'You give me enough money to go off to the South of France for a couple of weeks to write it. Meantime, Peter finds the money to make it.'

Val Guest had an impressive track record stretching back to 1942 and his first film, a short called *The Nose Has It*. He had directed the *Just William* comedies, as well as *Life With the Lyons* starring Ben, Bebe and Barbara. Without blinking, Frankie acquiesced. 'He was desperate to get into films,' recalls Peter Noble. 'Val had confidence in him. It was a marriage waiting to be consummated!'

Strictly on the artistic level only. Val was married to the lovely Yolande Donlan. Frankie was worrying himself sick that the world would find out about his gay tendencies. 'He was scared stiff that people would hear about it, and asked me what he should do.' Peter Noble recalls the comic's anguish. 'Frankie was a lovely guy, a nice jolly fellow full of indecision. Today it wouldn't matter, but in those days it could have ruined his career. All I could tell him was: keep it discreet!'

The film worked. An impressive cast was assembled. Petula Clark and Peter's actress wife Marianne Stone were air hostesses. Blonde Belinda Lee and raven-haired Lisa Gastoni were hired for glamour. George Coulouris was the villain.

Peter Noble, suddenly sporting the impressive title of Associate Producer, hawked the project around Wardour Street, and finally came up trumps with Eros Films. Their managing director Phil Hyams warned: 'We'll back you, but keep it under £50,000. OK?' OK it was. They shot it in three incredibly short weeks in an old bus garage in Southall, grandly renamed Southall Film Studios for the occasion. And brought it in at £40,000. The picture has been reissued six times, and was among the top earners in Eros's modest history.

Frankie was left with two memories of his screen debut. The last day saw sudden panic around the camera crew. Someone had done a spot of smart addition and found they were three minutes short of the compulsory seventy-five minutes to qualify it as a feature. If it wasn't the right length, it wouldn't get into the West End.

They only had the 'studio' for another half-hour. Val Guest was frantic. 'What do we do?' he demanded. 'How can we fill three minutes?'

Three minutes can be an awful long time on screen, twice as long as an average sequence, and three pages of a script. Frankie thought quickly. 'I've got an idea.' He had spotted a phone booth in one corner among the props. 'Put me in a phone-box, and I'll adlib a call to my old grandmother. Don't worry. I can do it.'

He did, too. Remember that, won't you, next time the *Runaway Bus* looms out of the swirling fog on your TV screens, most likely in the wee small hours. That desperate three-minute phone call from Percy Lamb to his old granny saved the day.

The second important factor for Frankie was that it proved his ticket to ride into the sights of the Rank Organization. Once alerted, they realized that in this stuttering incompetent they might have a potential star at their fingertips, maybe even another Norman Wisdom.

Alas, it was not to be. As so often in the celluloid world of broken dreams, the Rank supremo Earl St John and his accolytes had second thoughts. The following year Frankie was signed for a farce entitled *An Alligator Named Daisy*, but apparently it was not love at first bite between them. He was relegated to a supporting, nay, cameo role, in a fatuous comedy about a young songwriter (Donald Sinden) saddled with a pet alligator.

Frankie popped up again in *The Ladykillers*, a 1955 Ealing comedy featuring Alec Guinness's spooky villain plotting to murder an aged landlady, but getting his comeuppance from the wily victim. Frankie managed a 'blink-and-you-miss-me' appearance on the street. To complete a trio of unremarkable screen roles in that same year he made *Jumping for Joy*, playing a dog-track attendant at the White City who buys a greyhound — and does rather better with it than Ernie Wise's Short Fat Hairy Legs. At least Frankie was credited with 'an assured and pleasant performance' by the *Monthly Film Bulletin*.

Films like *A Touch of the Sun* (1956), dismissed as 'a ponderous comedy vehicle for Frankie Howerd' by one critic, *Watch It, Sailor* (1961) and *The Fast Lady* (1962) did little to enhance his reputation. Frankie wondered long and loud why nobody had the vision to build films around him 'Like they do in America for Bob Hope and Danny Kaye or in France for Fernandel.'

The truth was simple, if unpalatable. Frankie Howerd was no comedy actor, however hard he tried to prove otherwise. What he needed was the right vehicle to exploit his unique capacity to communicate directly with the viewers, whether winning their sympathy or playing King Leer.

Ray Galton is one close observer who was in no two minds about it. 'Let's face it, Frankie was a rotten actor,' he declares. 'He was terrible! The only way you could write for him and make it work was to put him in contact with the audience.

'That's how we approached him every time — we were writing for a personality who was already there. We didn't try to invent a character. We didn't have to. Frankie was all right when he could raise his eyebrows and pull faces, and as a comic he was a genius without any doubt. But he was hopeless when he tried to submerge all that into another role.'

After a moderate success with *Further Up the Creek* (1958) — 'I said Creek, madam, not Greek!' as Frankie pointed out at a reception shortly after — he found himself entangled in a ludicrous spoof on Gilbert and Sullivan called *The Cool Mikado* (1962), which the Cinematograph Exhibitors Association report dismissed rather kindly as 'feeble'. It was so bad that it doesn't even appear on Frankie's official biographical details issued to the media, and he always preferred not to discuss it.

When prodded, he recalls frantic days on the set with the director Michael Winner, and a script with lines he said came out of a Marx Brothers' comedy. *'Waiter, do you serve wild duck here?'* — *'No sir.'* — *'Well, bring me a tame one and I'll irritate it!'* The cast of stalwarts included Bernie Winters, Pete Murray and Burt Kwouk — who went on to make his name as the long-suffering Cato in the *Pink Panther* series, none of whom actually saw the film.

Frankie was not happy with anything about that experience, including its director. Indeed, at his favourite Italian trattoria, the Al Gallo D'Oro in Kensington — where Winner has been known to dine — he said to the restaurateur Tony Malvasi: 'If that fellow Winner comes in here, sit him as far away from me as possible!' It only happened once, and the two sat at opposite ends of the trattoria, studiously avoiding one another.

Frankie had little more than 'Cheese' to say in another weak comedy *The Mouse on the Moon* (1963), a spin-off from the 1953 Peter Sellers effort *The Mouse that Roared*. In this one the tiny duchy of Grand Fenwick discovers its home-made wine makes an explosive rocket fuel — but Frankie's role was burned-out almost before it began.

But if *The Runaway Bus* was the vehicle that launched his screen career, the film that took it another precious rung up the ladder was *The Great St Trinian's Train Robbery* in 1965. Surrounded by the gymslip terrors from Ronald Searle's fiendish imagination, he was cast as an inept trainee train robber, with the loot inevitably ending up hidden away in the school. Frankie and the gang meet their match in a pitched battle of eggs, flour and ripe tomatoes — a scene filmed with noisy exuberance at Shepperton Studios, and prompting the battered comic to say loudly and feelingly after the cameras stopped rolling: 'The trouble with child actors is that they tend to get carried away. And as far as I'm concerned, the further the better.' One consolation: the critics thought he was the best thing in it.

In 1968 Frankie Howerd made the shrewdest move of his somewhat lethargic screen career.

He joined the *Carry On* crowd.

Imagine a series of saucy seaside postcards come to vulgar, unabashed life, and you've got the *Carry On* phenomenon in a nutshell. The farcical comedies began life in 1958 with *Carry On Sergeant*, filmed in black and white at a cost of £74,000, with the likes of Kenneth Williams, Charles Hawtrey and Hattie Jacques trampling through the script with unrestrained glee. The public loved it. Thirty-four years and thirty films later the 'old firm' of producers Peter Rogers and director Gerald Thomas could still be found at Pinewood Studios on yet another saga, *Carry On Columbus*, doing their bit for Britain to celebrate the ancient mariner's epic voyage. Or something like that.

Peter, balding and urbane, prided himself on being the headmaster controlling a crowd of unruly pupils. A veteran of more than one hundred films, Rogers hid a sharp business brain beneath that avuncular image, and acted as a father confessor to any of his brood who needed advice or reassurance.

Gerald Thomas was equally laid back − on the surface. In reality his alert brown eyes never missed a trick. An old hand at the game, he had entered the industry as an assistant director on films like Laurence Olivier's *Hamlet* (1948) and a year later was associate editor on *The Third Man*.

The relaxed atmosphere on a *Carry On* set was legendary − and deliberate. Some directors, like the fearsome Otto Preminger, thrived on tension. Gerald Thomas strives for the opposite − 'When the red light isn't on, the whole set is like a dormitory feast. And it's all spontaneous.' He has been known to play the occasional practical joke on his cast, like filling Joan Sims' glass with neat gin instead of water for a drunk scene. His most famous remark on three decades of making the *Carry Ons*: 'It's not like work − it's a holiday.'

It was into this atmosphere that Frankie walked, with a certain trepidation, early one spring morning in 1968 to report for duty on the set of *Carry On Doctor*. If the butterflies were extra busy that first day, at least he knew he could not have been in better hands.

Pinewood is arguably the world's most elegant film studio, a converted Georgian mansion set in ninety acres of leafy Buckinghamshire countryside. The panelled restaurant serves food as fine as any West End emporium. The bar where Peter Rogers had his own corner to entertain friends was a popular watering hole in which to jostle shoulders with the famous.

Frankie bumped into Peter in the car park beside the front lawn as he made for his dressing-room. He noticed the producer was limping with the aid of a stick, after spraining his ankle in his garden. 'Hullo,' the new arrival greeted his new boss. 'What did you do − trip over your wallet?'

Peter took it rather well as an opening remark, but a chagrined Francis was heard to mutter in the bar that evening: 'Oh, Gawd! I don't know what came over me. I just said it . . .'

In fact, with half a century of screen laughter behind him, Peter Rogers is as likely to make his guests fall about as any of the professional comics he employs.

One anecdote that had Frankie's hangdog features twitching revolved around the time Peter and his wife Betty Box decided to spend Christmas in Venice. There they found themselves dinner guests of a director of the famous Gritti Palace Hotel. The executive's Italian wife − a devout Catholic − tapped the seat beside her and demanded imperiously: 'Peter, come and sit next to me and make me laugh!'

Not always easy, on cue. But Peter rose to the occasion. 'I wondered if I should use some form of manual dexterity,' he told Frankie. 'But I decided against it. Instead I asked her if she had heard the Pope's Christmas message.

'She said she hadn't.

'So I told her: "The Pope's Christmas message is: *'Don't come, all ye faithful!'* " And she never spoke to me for the rest of the meal . . .'

A revealing insight into how a film company prepared for the arrival of a stuttering loon in its midst is provided by Peter Rogers. The script, for instance. You might expect it to be full of 'ooohs' and 'aaahs' to make the purveyor of these sounds more at home. It was not. 'This is something we have always stopped scriptwriters trying to do,' Rogers declares emphatically. 'They come to me and say: "Who's playing this? Ah − Frankie Howerd. We'll put in an 'oooh' here and an 'aaah' there, along with the occasional 'Not on your Nellie!' to round things off."

'And I tell them: "Oh no you won't! Don't worry who's playing it. That's our problem, not yours. Just write the bloody scenes!" We'll cast them, and if the artists are any good they will get the best out of it. If Frankie Howerd wants to put in his exclamations, he'll know when and where. It's the same as trying to script Jack Douglas's twitch . . . You just can't!'

Carry On Doctor was the fourteenth in the series that had plugged into the nation's funny-bone, and survived the vitriol of the critics to become part of Britain's screen heritage. It was written by Talbot Rothwell, who would be responsible for twenty in all, and in 1977 was awarded the OBE for charity work — the laughter he had brought to millions was not cited. Mindful of the daffodil gag, 'Tolly' added the subtitle to his film: *If you say it's a thermometer I'll have to believe you, but it's a funny place to put it.*

Frankie Howerd as Francis Bigger would hold his audience enthralled with such profundities as: 'What is mind? No matter. What is matter? Never mind.'

He is a patient in a hospital where popular and romantic Dr Kilmore (Jim Dale) has been given the sack after being caught in a compromising position on the roof of the nurses' home. The patients are determined to get him reinstated, and rise up in revolt against formidable Matron (step forward again the indomitable Hattie Jacques, the epitome of dragon-lady matrons) and sarcastic Dr Tinkle (Kenneth Williams in his supercilious element).

The *Carry On* team were out in force: Sid James, covertly smoking under the bedcovers, Bernard Bresslaw with his foot encased in plaster, Charles Hawtrey suffering a sympathetic pregnancy, Barbara Windsor sending the temperatures soaring.

Joan Sims plays Bigger's mousy assistant whose deafness is the butt of many a cruel joke. The finale has the rebellious patients strapping Dr Tinkle to the operating table and waving various sharpened scalpels in the direction of his lower regions. The knives don't scare him — but the threat of an enema forces him to yield and bring Dr Kilmore back. Cheers all round.

Although welcomed into the fold with open arms, Frankie remained the odd man out, just that bit removed from the off-set fun and games. Lost in his own world, with the clouds of self-doubt hovering over him during the hours before a major scene, he would stay in his dressing-room or be spotted wandering alone around the sets that make up the huge Pinewood complex.

It wasn't that he was playing the big star, as some unkindly suggested. Merely that he was keeping to himself. Gerald Thomas recalls the early days as Frankie got used to being the new boy in the family: 'He was an individual, a loner. He would sit in a corner just reading quietly, but he was always very polite if people came up to him.'

For a hospital farce, Thomas was the ideal director. After all, he had studied to be a doctor in his native Hull before chucking in his stethoscope and turning to a different kind of cutting-room.

One dilemma that caused a spot of head-scratching was when Peter and Gerald realized they had two camp comics in the same film. They solved it by the simple means of making sure the pair never appeared in a scene together. 'One would have eclipsed the other,' says Peter. 'It's a shame, but we couldn't risk it.'

They were probably right, though one can only wonder at what would have happened if the pair had been unleashed on one another – on the screen, that is. Kenneth Williams died in 1988, aged sixty-two, and the world was deprived of another outrageous talent. His own catch phrase was 'Stop messing about', and on the set he would regale the crew with a stream of anecdotes and impersonations that anyone would have paid good money to see.

Some lines in the *Carry On* sagas could have been uttered by either of them – such as Kenneth's famous last words as Caesar, on the point of assassination: 'Infamy! Infamy! They've all got it in for me!'

Nostril-flaring and eye-popping on screen, Kenneth Williams shared with Frankie one other trait: behind the mask of laughter lay a complex and self-absorbed personality, coupled with a high intelligence and a remarkable knowledge of history and literature.

Frankie's second foray into *Carry On* territory came two years later. *Carry On Up the Jungle* was once again filmed in darkest Pinewood, and once again the plot was hardly one to tax the grey matter. Lady Evelyn Bagley (Joan Sims at her most imperious) joins an expedition into Africa to seek her long-lost son. Frankie played Professor Inigo Tinkle (possibly a distant relation of Dr Tinkle), searching for the legendary oozalum bird, along with his inept assistant Claude Chumley (Kenneth Connor). Fearless white hunter Bill Boosey (Sid James) is searching for anything in a skirt.

The gang was virtually all there. Another relative newcomer played Jungle Boy Tarzan – a pudgy Terry Scott, complete with yell and loin-cloth, swinging from mangy ropes and crashing through rotting branches, ignoring too late the warning signs: *Danger – Concealed Tree.*

As the batty ornithologist, Frankie filled the role that would have been reserved for that other master of innuendo, Kenneth Williams, who had other commitments. The script was pure − or impure − Francis. His conversation oozed with earnest erudition. Told about a snake that rocks its head repeatedly from side to side, he promptly identified it as 'a harmless Vindscreen Viper'.

Asked why giraffes have such long necks he has a ready explanation. 'It's quite simple. It's because their heads are so far from their bodies.' Indeed so.

Gerald Thomas applied his customary patience with his nervous star. 'I wouldn't tell Frankie how to do a scene. I would take him on to the set and we would go through it, just as it was written. I would look at his interpretation and tell him if I thought anything was wrong.

'Sometimes he would be projecting too hard − as if he was in cabaret or on a stage. He forgot that on the big screen your reactions, your glances and your "oohs" and "aahs" have to come down. Too often Frankie was giving a performance to an audience, not to a camera. But he very quickly cottoned on, and accepted my criticisms one hundred per cent. Then he did what *he* wanted!'

Gerald Thomas speaks half-jokingly, but there is more than a grain of truth in this last remark. Frankie's own personality took over any role in which he was cast, as a second look at his films testifies. In *Doctor* he was Frankie in a hospital bed − home from home for a self-confessed hypochondriac. In *Jungle* he was Frankie in a pith helmet. 'Whatever you played Frankie in, he remained Frankie Howerd.'

He also remained faithful to his old tricks. Down in the jungle something was stirring, and it was only a matter of time − about two days − before the film unit were referring to him (strictly behind his back, of course) as the African Queen. Film studios can be very bitchy places.

A few years later Gerald Thomas would direct him for the small screen with a *Carry On* Christmas special for Thames TV, with an audience. Gerald noticed the difference immediately. 'Frankie missed an audience, no question about it. But on our film set when the crew started laughing − that's when he relaxed.'

In between fighting off insects, rampant gorillas and cannibals heating up the cooking-pot, the Professor has to repel the amorous efforts of Lady Evelyn to lure him into her tent. Not to mention avoiding the giant piles of you-know-what left wherever an elephant has set foot, which provides a running gag throughout the picture.

Add Charles Hawtrey as the Great Tonka leading a tribe of female Amazons from Afrodosia, and you have a recipe for the usual below-the-belt jokes and belly laughs.

Probably the best gag of all is when the Professor and his sidekick find the oozalum bird and return home in triumph with the wretched captive in its cage. The highlight of his lecture to the Royal Geographical Society will be when he unveils the cage containing the rare bird. There are gasps when Prof Tinkle whips off the cloth − only to find the bird has performed its unique and celebrated trick. 'Where's it disappeared to?' he cries, open-mouthed. A question mercifully left unanswered.

Gerald Thomas remembers how fastidious Frankie was for this final scene. 'He wore a velvet smoking-jacket that had to be brushed every time he stepped in front of the cameras. He was the only man I knew who had dandruff in his hairpiece!'

There is an old joke about the actor who fished in his wallet and pulled out a green-back. It was a coin. But unlike many in his profession who were notorious 'tight-wads', Frankie usually paid his round. You don't need to be a psychologist to determine why so many show business celebrities are known for their care with money. The hard statistic to swallow is that at any given moment ninety-five per cent of actors are out of work. For even the rich and famous, the branding-iron of the dole queue has burned in so deep they tend to be overly protective of their wealth.

Frankie, mindful of the hard slog in the days of theatrical digs and gas-fire boarding houses, was careful − but not mean. On the other hand, he knew when a free drink was going begging.

Producer Kevin Francis remembers a lunchtime in the bar at Pinewood, that most cheery and welcoming of studio 'clubs' where you could be pretty sure of spying a familiar face.

Frankie was filming *Jungle*, and appeared in the doorway resplendent in the tropical regalia of Professor Tinkle. After a morning in pursuit of the infamous oozalum bird, he approached the bar and hailed Kevin.

'Is his Lordship around?' he queried. That meant Peter Rogers.

'No, you missed him by five minutes,' Kevin replied.

'Ah,' said Frankie. He thought for a moment. 'Wait a minute,' he said. 'I know you've got nothing to do with the *Carry Ons* — but aren't you director of another company where he's the chairman?'

'Yes, that's right.' It was the one connected with TV spin-offs.

'Well,' said Frankie airily. 'That'll do then. I only came in here for a free drink. If I can't get one off him direct, I'll get it from you by proxy!'

And he did it with a totally straight face, as the others in the group chuckled — and Kevin reached for his wallet.

Sadly, Frankie Howerd was never able to climb aboard the good ship *Santa Maria* for *Carry On Columbus*, which began filming the day after he went into hospital for the last time. Both Peter and Gerald wanted him to play the King of Spain, with Joan Sims as Queen Isabella, and they would have made a splendid pair. 'It would have been wonderful,' says Peter. 'They worked so well together.' Leslie Phillips, regarded as another central member of the *Carry On* cast — though he had only appeared in three of them — donned the King's robes instead.

A month before the cameras were due to roll, Frankie's agent Tessa Le Bars phoned through to the production office and spoke to Gerald Thomas.

'Gerald,' she said quietly, 'If I were you, I would re-cast.'

Thomas heard the news of Frankie's death when he reached his Buckinghamshire home at the end of the day's filming on *Columbus*. His tribute was immediate and heartfelt. 'I felt a terrible sense of loss — even though it was expected. I liked him as a man, even though I think he was a sad man for much of his life. I shall miss him.

'But let's not forget Frankie had a good, full life before the knock sounded. It was a great innings.'

Frankie Howerd did his best, but he was never destined to be a great movie star. The film for which he is best remembered followed his last *Carry On*, and was again written by Talbot Rothwell. *Up Pompeii* was spawned by the TV series of the same name, which in turn had come about as a result of Frankie's stage success in *A Funny Thing Happened on the Way to the Forum*.

Such chain reactions are not uncommon in show business, but they don't often happen to a Roman slave.

In *Forum* he was Pseudolus, leering out at the audience from in front of the curtain to confide the naughty goings-on in ancient Rome as only Frankie could. In *Up Pompeii* he was Lurgius, conniving slave at the Court of Nero, bartering scantily-clad slave girls for various favours for his master.

Frankie was in rampant form. '*E-lix-ir, she said. Straight out. The highest hips in the business, she's got. Then without so much as a by-your-leave or kiss your asp, she pushed this cup of pop in my mush. I tell you not a lie. Pompeii's kinkier than Rome. But what about that Nero − didn't he do funny things with faggots. Like burning things . . . Eh? Oooh . . . aaah . . . Naughty?*'

The film was most notable for the performance of studied boredom by Patrick Cargill as the Emperor, and for the kind of dialogue that threw up lines like: 'Hey, there − orgy girl!' The statuesque Valerie Leon remembers her own one liner, 'You can call me Daili.' To which the dreaded Lurgius responds: 'I'd rather call you nightly . . .'

But the film was a box-office hit, and Frankie found his fame followed him overseas. On holiday in Tenerife, a man bent his ear in a local flamenco bar telling him how much he enjoyed the film − and going through the plot, virtually line by line. After half an hour Frankie had lost interest and was looking decidedly bored.

'What's the matter?' asked the man. 'Don't you want to talk about it?'

Frankie inquired: 'What do you do for a living?'

'I'm a butcher,' said the barfly.

Frankie said tartly: 'Do you want to talk about meat?' End of conversation. And, possibly, end of a fan too.

Predictably, there was a sequel − and then another. *Up the Chastity Belt* promoted Frankie into the role of Sir Lurkalot, bound for the Crusades. He falls foul of Robin Hood and a band of very gay Merry Men. The jokes were suitably lavatorial − a flash in the pan, as someone remarked − and the critics gave it a surprisingly enthusiastic thumbs-up. Their main concern was with the sexual frolickings between Frankie and Eartha Kitt — 'uncomfortable close-ups,' said the *Monthly Film Bulletin*. But they threw him the bouquet: 'Howerd is bitingly funny.'

The *Times* pronounced the film 'quite a bit funnier than its predecessor', and hailed Frankie as 'still greater than the sum of his parts.' The private kind, presumably.

The third in this oddball trilogy was *Up the Front*, set in occupied France in 1914, with our Francis cast as Private Lurk, an ex-bandboy 'on whose rearguard action' (oh dear!) the fate of England depends. Directed by his old chum Ned Sherrin and featuring another old friend Zsa Zsa Gabor, the film was described as 'a load of old military tattoo'. 'Nuff said?

Like all comics with genius in their veins, Frankie knew exactly what he wanted from his writers. 'I can't stand filth. Dirty jokes always embarrass me. But vulgarity is a good thing. Life is vulgar. The human body is terribly vulgar — it has to be to keep healthy! I'm not a blue comic — in fact up north I've been asked to make my act bluer!'

Even those who flinched at the rudery of *Up Pompeii* were given their answer: 'It was vulgar without being dirty. There's a lot of talk about orgies, but it's all talk. Anyway, the worst thing about orgies is that you don't know who to thank afterwards!'

Frankie allowed himself a wry smile. 'Did you know that the *Catholic Herald* thought the TV series was morally very clean? If anyone was offended, it was because the jokes were played out against skimpily-clad girls. If we'd done it in modern times, all dressed in old macs, nobody would have complained.'

The rare jokes he did tell had more than a hint of black comedy about them. Like the man who was shipwrecked with his dog and was washed up on a desert island. '*After a week the man cooked his pet, ate it, then sat back and looked at the remains. "What a shame," he said. "Fido would have loved those bones!"* '

Indeed, even in his Army days Frankie never fell into the temptation of following the other lads in barrack-room language. Ingrained into him was a childhood memory of how, at the tender age of five, he had overheard the milkman on his rounds in Arbroath Road give vent to *the* four-letter word when he dropped a bottle on the pavement. Without any idea of what it meant, little Francis innocently repeated it that night over supper. His horrified mother immediately clipped his ear — hard enough for Frankie to do the crying over spilt milk. But he never swore again. The only four-letter word he used in his act was 'piss' (as in 'off'), and that was carefully chosen for maximum effect and least offence. Plus the occasional 'bugger'.

His promoter pal Lew Lane declares: 'Frankie didn't like swearing, and he didn't need to indulge in it in order to get laughs. It was all innuendo and double meanings, and things left hanging in the air. He was a master of it. Our vulgar minds did the rest!'

The House in Nightmare Park (1973) was a comedy suspense yarn devised by Clive Exton and Terry Nation, two old hands at TV thrillers. Frankie was type-cast (his own words) as a ham actor who falls heir to a family fortune. He foolishly accepts an invitation from his wicked uncle (Ray Milland) to an old dark house where he can be bumped off at leisure so that Uncle can grab the pickings. The director of what turned out to be a neat little thriller was Peter Sykes (no relation to Eric), an Australian anxious to establish a track record for himself. He enthusiastically put Frankie through an obstacle course of swamps, chases, falls down staircases — 'Memories of my infancy' — and a climax in a pit filled with snakes. Milland played his role as a mad axe-man with zest. Frankie kept his nerve, but sweated away half a stone in the course of filming. The reviews proved well worth the effort, and the film was a modest success at the box-office.

Frankie finally made it to Hollywood in 1978. In hindsight, perhaps he should have stayed at home. But he was given The Treatment: a first-class ticket, a luxury villa complete with pool, a chauffeured limousine to ferry him back and forth to Universal Studios, *and* he got to meet Rock Hudson.

The film was *Sergeant Pepper's Lonely Hearts Club Band*, produced by Robert Stigwood, with a hotchpotch cast varying from Alice Cooper to Steve Martin. It is best forgotten, and quickly was.

As a £6-million hype for the Beatles' record, featuring twenty-nine of their songs, it aroused a brief overnight interest, but the adventures of a family band — the Bee Gees, with Peter Frampton

— were too quirky to make major waves.

Frankie was cast in the unlikely role of a villain and it fitted him badly. Mean Mister Mustard was a computer expert who fancied a girl called Strawberry Fields, and wanted to take over the world as an incidental bonus. Frankie would sum up the experience: 'I only got the Mustard role because they couldn't get Ronald Colman. But who can resist Hollywood? So I went.' He did sing 'When I'm Sixty-Four', and although he had three years to go, it was one for the record. He also put the word around the studio that he was an Earl, and actually had some of the gatemen calling him 'Your Lordship' when he was driven through. 'Cheeky git, wasn't I?'

At least Francis had tasted the good life, Hollywood style. But whoops! That fickle finger again — pointing his way.

Frankie didn't know it, but he was on the brink of another slide down the slippery slope he feared most.

12

Bottoms Up!

'Come on, Frankie, show us your Bottom!' The cry went up on the stage of the Old Vic as Francis Howerd, classical actor, arrived on an overcast Monday morning in February 1958 to join the Royal Shakespeare Company, the most élite acting ensemble in the country.

In the Tit and Bum Show, no less.

Let us be accurate. Oh yes, accurate we must be. The cry was more a concerted stage whisper from the thespians gathered under the hallowed arches of the historic corner theatre opposite Waterloo Station. And the play was *A Midsummer Night's Dream* – known to the acting fraternity as the T. and B. Show because it's the one with Titania and Bottom in it.

And Frankie Howerd was playing Bottom the Weaver to make it the Titter and Bum Show . . .

With a stroke of inspiration – the doubters called it sheer lunacy – director Michael Benthall had seen in Frankie's mournful countenance some hint of the quality that might make his face a memorable Bottom. When the call came, he thought they were joking. But when asked somewhat curtly if he would rather play Oberon, King of the Fairies, Frankie plumped hurriedly for Bottom. Even at the serf's rate of £30 per week.

The rest of the Company were not so sure. Headed by Joyce Redman, Edward Hardwicke, Moira Shearer as Titania, Paul Daneman, Ronald Fraser and Coral Browne, they were dumbfounded when they heard the news of a vulgarian stand-up comic about to share the stage with them.

Gathered in a semi-circle on the stage with their scripts, they awaited with some apprehension the arrival of their newest member for the first day of rehearsals. What Francis had confided to his media friends hadn't helped. 'Can't go wrong!' he said. 'It's a good script. A very successful man is that Mr W. Shakespeare. Dead, you know, that's the trouble.

'But he might have written this script for me. I'm sure he had

someone like me in mind. I've often been described as The End,
but this Bottom gag is no help at all to a comic trying to go
straight.'

The rest of the cast got the gag over and done with in the first
minute, and prepared to welcome the new Bottom.

Margaret Courtenay, who would become part of Frankie's inner
circle of friends, was playing Hippolata. A seasoned RSC actress,
she recalls his arrival. 'Frankie came out on to the stage, rather
shyly. We were all standing around in a circle clutching our scripts.
We looked at each other — because Frankie wasn't holding one.
I mean, when you're in a company like the Royal Shakespeare
and you're doing maybe five plays a year — you can't be without
a script on the first day! But he was. And when he started on
his lines he was word perfect.'

No mean feat for a comic thrown into the lion's den in such
august company — even if it was February. Particularly with
intimidating set speeches to get through like the famous awakening
monologue in Act IV Scene I which runs to 193 words. Frankie
declaimed it like a veteran of the Bard: '*When my cue comes,
call me and I will answer* —'

'He was marvellous,' says Maggie. 'We couldn't believe how
serious he was. But he did shake us all up a bit when he got to
the death scene, stuck a sword under his arm, and fell to the
ground . . .'

In the play-within-a-play Bottom, now cast as Pyramus, thrusts
the sword into his body uttering the words:

> 'Now am I dead,
> Now am I fled;
> My soul is in the sky:
> Tongue, lose thy light!
> Moon, take thy flight!
> Now die, die, die, die, die.'

And so he dies.

But instead of saying '*Die!*' as the script demanded, Frankie
rolled around the boards clutching the sword to his chest and
shouting: '*Di-diddle-ee-ay-tay!*'

Maggie still shudders quietly at the memory of the circle of
stunned faces on the Old Vic stage. 'He sat up with a perfectly

With his old pal Tommy
Cooper – two clowns
together imitating
the Eiffel Tower.
Or maybe
they've just got a
leaning towards
each other

Tea and sympathy at home. When the going got rough, the friends flocked to help

Another cuppa abroad – flying the flag with yet another morale boosting show for the troops

And now Frankie's awash with tea – getting the full Hollywood treatment in his American screen debut *Sergeant Pepper's Lonely Hearts Club Band* (1978). Along with the pool came a house and a chauffeur-driven limousine

A scene from *Sergeant Pepper*, with Frankie playing Mean Mister Mustard, a lovable rogue

Socializing with Edward Heath…

… and with Dr David Owen and his wife, Deborah

Old world courtesy for the Duchess of Kent, who seems not entirely displeased. Ernie Wise smiles approval

Whatever Malcolm McDowell
said, Frankie was *a-mazed*!

And Cynthia Payne – was it
'Call me Madam'…?

Left: Bursting with pride, as he becomes Frankie Howerd OBE. The date was 2 March 1977

Below: *Up Pompeii* was so popular that in 1991 Frankie was persuaded to don his toga again as leering Lurcio for a TV special – twenty years on. But oh no, missus! The expression hasn't changed

Right: The last picture. Frankie is given a chocolate Easter bunny and a kiss from Sister Louise Verity as he leaves Harley Street clinic on 14 April 1992. But he had gone home knowing his days were numbered

Below: The funeral in a Somerset churchyard – and Cilla Black weeps for her old friend

serious expression and asked: "How was that?"

'We had to explain to him − well, it's not quite what is expected . . . But of course, he was having us all on. And every time after that when we came to that scene in the public performances, we wondered if he might just . . .'

Frankie didn't. He controlled himself − and the reviews next morning hinted at a new star born into the Royal Shakespeare Company's firmament.

It was, said Frankie Howerd at the time, all part of a Master Plan. 'It's what I call my transition period. I'm slowly changing from Frankie the variety comic to Francis the comedy actor.' The trouble was, he meant it.

At least one good-luck telegram on opening night reminded him of his grass roots: *'Here's to a warm hand on your opening'* it said, signed *Anon*. Francis never knew who sent it and his anonymous fan never owned up.

Was Francis needing a new size in hats? Listen to him regaling a rapt audience with his opinion of the Bard: 'The only thing about Shakespeare is that he did not understand the art of the throwaway line. Every single word I utter has to be delivered in well-*rounded* tones. Do you see?' Mind you, he was happy with the RSC crowd. 'They're very kind to me here. Not a bit arty-crafty . . .'

And he got the royal seal of approval, with a charity gala performance of scenes from *Dream* before the Queen − and a backstage presentation afterwards, with compliments flowing as he shook the royal hand. The photographs went round the world.

Frankie's Master Plan had been forged after his success in *Charley's Aunt* in 1956. The Globe Theatre had been packed out, and the *Observer* review heralded 'An historic stroke of miscasting has produced a performance which could and should run for several years.' They were talking about Frankie, enjoying himself hugely as Lord Fancourt Balberley, arraigned against Gerald Harper, suitably lecherous as the master of the house.

Frankie had made his first TV appearance on 11 January 1952 with his own *Howerd Crowd*, backed by the blonde and bubbly singing trio of the Beverley Sisters. But the culture vulture had Frankie firmly in its claws. While he kept the popularity pot bubbling with TV appearances and the occasional series, Francis was chasing other shadows. He tried his hand at a spot of Molière, playing a bald-headed old coot in *The School for Wives*, which did him no good at all with his public.

Then came an offer to star in a musical called *Mr Venus,* about an alien who arrives from Venus to preach love and understanding on our wicked planet. He uses a publican (that's Frankie) to spread the good tidings. The show hit problems from the outset, and the sight of Anton Diffring as the Winged Messenger parading around the stage in a sequined jockstrap, high boots and plastic wings did little to help the production. Frankie tried to give it some sense of direction, even bringing in fresh scriptwriters as a panic last measure. But the show had hit the iceberg and sank ignominiously.

Mr Venus closed on 8 November 1958 after a lamentable sixteen-day run at the Prince of Wales. Frankie gathered his dignity and his wits around him as best he could, and conceded: 'It was doomed from the start. It's distressing to be in a flop. Very distressing.' But he got good notices – 'Among the best I've ever had. Particularly in the, you know, *intellectual* papers.'

But he also vented his spleen on those who could see no further than the nearest titter. 'If Olivier plays a music hall comic, everyone says: "Isn't he clever?" But if a comedian tries to act, they say he's getting above himself.' It was a cry from the heart.

Friends rallied round and made all the right noises of sympathy, but in the end Frankie had to face his future alone. He moved house at this time, finding a small cottage in a mews in Napier Place off Kensington High Street, and furnishing it with his beloved antiques. His boxer dog Red had long since headed for the great kennel in the sky, and Frankie had only human company for solace.

Frankie took to wandering around the streets at night, muttering to himself – in fact he was rehearsing lines for his next show, but who was to know that? On one occasion a nervous old lady saw the hunched figure behaving like Hamlet on the battlements of Elsinore, and called the police. The local constabulary arrived to invite the miscreant to help them with their inquiries, only to end up asking Frankie for his autograph.

Later, when he bought a cottage near the Domesday village of Axbridge in Somerset, Frankie would actually rehearse in a neighbouring field, in front of an audience of cud-chewing cows.

Frankie's personal habits were certainly bordering on the eccentric. Callers at his home never knew quite what the condition of the place would be like — or the condition of its owner, either.

Actor Graham Stark, who had observed from close quarters the off-screen eccentricities of that other master of mirth Peter Sellers, thought he'd seen it all until he accepted an invitation to dine with Frankie at the mews cottage.

Graham received a phone call from the BBC asking him to present himself at the Howerd homestead with a copy of his script for the following week's *Frankie Howerd Show* on Radio 2, where he was appearing as one of the guests. Luncheon would be served, said the lady from the production office.

'I got myself all spruced up in my best suit, silver tie and stiff collar,' Stark recalls. 'I felt I should look my best if I was going to the star's private home. I was particularly *sprauncy* that day.' Graham has a way with descriptive words, even if they're not to be found in the Concise Oxford Dictionary.

'Frankie's friend Lee Young answered the door and I was taken straight through into the kitchen. There was Frankie in old corduroy trousers, carpet slippers — and a jumper with his elbow coming out of the sleeve! This was a man earning thousands, who looked as if he didn't have fourpence to his name.

'They sat me down at a rickety card-table in the middle of the kitchen, and some old crone with a cigarette hanging out of her mouth was shuffling around by the gas stove not more than four feet away from my head, banging away with pots and pans and making the most enormous clatter.

'Finally she appeared next to us with the fag still drooping from her mouth, and up-ended a saucepan with a frightful brown mess in it all over my plate. I think it passed for stew. I nearly passed out after tasting it.

'Lee had a floral waistcoat on, and he was obviously very proud ot it. "What do you think?" he asked. "Nice and colourful isn't it?"

' "It makes you look like a ponce!" Frankie growled.

' "That's all right then," said Lee happily.'

Graham spent three hours poring over the script on that wobbly card-table in 'Dickensian surroundings', and remembers it as one of the strangest days of his life. Frankie didn't even open the Scotch.

He had been brilliant in *Charley's Aunt*. But think of a play starring Frankie Howerd, and you think of *A Funny Thing Happened on the Way to the Forum*.

This riotous Roman romp, with music and lyrics by Stephen Sondheim, of *West Side Story* fame, actually began life two hundred years before Christ, with the Roman playwright Titus Maccius Plautus (254–184 BC). From the Umbrian village of Sarsina, Plautus took the road to Rome – and twenty-one of his comedies survived to remain classics in their field. Burt Shevelove and Larry Gelbart had combined on the story, and assembled a supporting cast of ignoble Romans headed by Robertson Hare, Kenneth Connor, Jon Pertwee and Isla Blair.

It opened in the West End on 3 October 1963, and Frankie instinctively knew he would be occupying the star dressing-room at the Strand Theatre for a very long time. It was, he said, 'The start of my slavish period.'

The sweet smell of success is a heady aroma, and his nostrils were filled with it as the curtain rang down on the first night and the audience rose as one man to applaud him. Frankie was so overcome he had to retreat to his dressing-room, lock the door, and cry his heart out for ten minutes before he could regain his composure to meet the wellwishers and pop the champagne corks. 'It was the most moving night of my whole life,' he said later.

His instincts were right. The critics raved. They called him 'The star who came back to brilliance' . . . 'Our most original droll'. And, in the *Times*: 'That preposterous Cupid, that angel in a huff, that maiden uncle . . .' A little over the top, perhaps, but Frankie thought of framing it.

The preposterous Cupid was the conniving slave Pseudolus, and he came out to face his audience before the curtain had even risen. In a ludicrous pale blue combination-type garment with stripes of knitting all over it, he looked more like a circus clown who had lost his way than a slave from ancient Rome.

He listened – for once – to his director. George Abbott was all of seventy-six, a veteran playwright, producer and sometime actor who in an impressive career had collaborated on the script of *All Quiet on the Western Front* and had directed two films of his own stage musicals, *Pajama Game* and *Damn Yankees*. A man not to be taken lightly, and even Frankie was overawed by someone who was such a part of stage and screen history. 'A very remote man,' was Frankie's assessment. 'Like a judge. But a brilliant director.'

George Abbot spelled it out in three crisp sentences. 'Stop trying to be funny. The words are funny. Believe in them, interpret them, just do it!'

Frankie did it. And, warm hand or not, the opening was right up his *Via*.

It was the kind of entrance Frankie had been making all his career, though never to announce a play, even one as wild and whacky as this toga-clad frolic. But the titters started at once, as he warmed up the audience with intimate revelations about the naughty goings-on behind the marble pillars.

The show ran until July 1965. After which Frankie took a much-needed holiday in the sun. In Beirut — in the good days.

If imitation is the sincerest form of flattery, then Frankie could feel complimented indeed. Not just because every comic across the land could mimic him — as with Tommy Cooper, you didn't even have to put a name to it. But the show itself would receive the ultimate kudos of spawning two television series and a film.

It took seven years, during which time Frankie's career would go into the doldrums yet again, before he next donned a toga for *Up Pompeii*. This particular dip was caused by being a slave to ambition, and a massive misjudgment in an attempt to conquer America.

The play was *The Wind in the Sassafras Tree* (1968), a spoof Western adapted by Galton and Simpson from a satire by the avant-garde French playwright René de Obaldia. The title alone should have warned him. Even with Ray and Alan in his corner, the play had the kiss of death on it for a stutterless Kansas dirt farmer named John Emery Rockefeller, the role Frankie took on.

One who escaped with her Press cuttings and reputation intact was Barbara Windsor. The script contained all the time-honoured clichés in the book, and with a big gun like David Merrick in the producer's saddle there were high hopes riding on it when it opened at the Belgrade Theatre in Coventry. Frankie spent most of his time in a log cabin smoking a clay pipe and doing his best to be witty rather than outrageous. The cast included a funny pioneer wife, a funny rebel son, a funny drunken doctor, a funny mysterious stranger, and a 'Come up and see me some time' saloon girl. No prizes for guessing who filled that costume part, in every sense and in all the right places.

Barbara Windsor recalls: 'I only had about ten minutes on stage – but I made the most of them and knocked their socks off! It brought the house down on opening night. We got a wonderful reception, and the reviews were marvellous.

'I thought everything was fine – but after the curtain came down and we were all celebrating in the bar Frankie behaved very strangely towards me. It turned out he was pissed off because I got more laughs than he did and he didn't speak to me for three days. He was actually sulking – and I was supposed to be his friend! But eventually he got over it, and we finished the run as if nothing had happened.'

The show never made it to the West End. Instead, American producer Arthur Lewis took over from Merrick for the US run, and Frankie found himself bound for Boston for the preview run with a new supporting cast, all of them with genuine 'Howdy yo'-all' accents. Barbara stayed home. She was committed to a TV series called *Wild Wild Women*, and reluctantly told Frankie: 'I'm sorry, love. I can't be with you in the States. But I'll keep my fingers crossed for you.'

It was the best thing for her – and the worst thing for him. In fact Barbara kept hidden from Frankie the ominous news that her agent had warned her against playing the role in the US. ' "Don't do it," he said. "Frankie is very British, and very eccentric. All those 'oohs' and 'aahs' – I'm not sure the Yanks are ready for him, or that he's ready for them!" And he was right. It was the best advice I could have had.'

Ray Galton is in no two minds about it. 'In America they didn't know his comedy. He wasn't a household name. They just thought he was an actor who couldn't act.'

The play opened in Boston to mixed reviews, went on to Washington, made it as far as Broadway – and closed. The date was 28 October 1968. It had lasted just one week. Frankie's chief memory of that disastrous episode was being accused of racism in a Boston newspaper.

The play, its critic alleged, was anti-American, ridiculing the ethnic minorities — and, worse, with a Britisher at the core of all the trouble. To a bewildered Frankie, it had seemed merely to be a harmless joke about cowboys and Indians. The only reservations he had envisaged were the kind where you found Redskins living in tepees.

Sadly he packed his bags and headed for home.

At least he did it in style, aboard the Queen Elizabeth on her last voyage. Frankie even gave the passengers an unheralded cabaret, starting off with the time-honoured *Titanic* gag: '*I know I asked for ice, waiter, but this is ridiculous!*' Tact was never Frankie's strong point, remember?

Tact? Any lingering doubt on that score would have been swiftly dispelled had you been present at the Press conference called to announce the ITV line-up for Christmas 1969. Perhaps too much of the seasonal spirit had got into Francis, who was one of the stars summoned along to the Mayfair Hotel to help the launch. Or perhaps it was just that he liked to shock people. But halfway through the proceedings Frankie rose from his seat in the small theatre and threw a question at the Big Five programme bosses gathered on the stage: Bill Ward (ATV), Brian Tesler (Thames TV), Cyril Bennett (LWT), David Plowright (Granada) and Donald Baverstock (Yorkshire).

''Ere, excuse me!' All heads turned. 'Can I ask how many of you gentlemen are going to resign by this time next year?' Laughter in the house. With five abstentions. Frankie never did explain exactly what he was getting at.

The years had done nothing to mellow Frankie. If anything, he became more petulant and demanding as his fame grew — and the ratings with it. David Hatch, a parson's son from Cheshire who would make it through the ranks of the BBC to become Managing Director of Network Radio, witnessed Frankie's mercurial moods at first hand.

In 1977 he was a Light Entertainment producer put in charge of *The Frankie Howerd Show*, a six-part sit-com series that would go out on Friday nights, 8.00 p.m. peak time. The Radio 2 bosses,

knowing their volatile star, needed someone with the right mix
of authority and kid gloves to handle him. Hatch, stocky and
tough, was the man.

'Frankie was not always the easiest of performers to get on
with,' he recalls, in something of an understatement. 'It was a
rich experience for me.'

The formula consisted of an opening monologue from Frankie
followed by a couple of sketches, often with June Whitfield as
his 'other half'.

'Frankie felt very secure with June,' Hatch recalls. 'We had
her in the show as often as we could.'

The show was recorded on Sunday nights at the Paris Theatre
near Piccadilly Circus, with a live audience. No question of canned
laughter. The red light went on at 7.00 p.m., and they would try
to get through on a straight run without too many hiccups and
re-runs to spoil the flow. Basically, it was like a proper theatre
show.

The pattern was always the same. The cast and production team
would arrive at 2.00 p.m. for rehearsals, and work right through
until 6.00 p.m. The doors opened at 6.30 p.m., and three hundred
and twenty people who had been patiently queueing for up to an
hour in Lower Regent Street would file in. The producer would
welcome them from the stage, and indulge in a spot of warm-up
patter to get them in the right mood. At 7.00 p.m. – Curtain Up.

Hatch had the first hint of what he was in for when the phone
rang at his home in Hounslow, Middlesex. Ten o'clock, Saturday
night. Just when he was thinking of reaching for the cocoa. The
show was going out next day.

Frankie was on the phone. 'I don't think it's going to work.
I don't like the opening monologue . . . I don't understand where
the jokes are.' His voice was glum, with a hint of desperation.
Then: 'Can you come round?'

He had had the script a week, been through it with a fine-tooth
comb, and passed it as A-OK.

Hatch said wearily: 'When?' But he knew the answer.

'Now, of course! We've got to get it right –'

Hounslow is fifteen miles from Edwardes Square, Kensington,
where Frankie was now in residence. Recalling it, Hatch sits in
his fourth floor office at Broadcasting House mulling over

memories of frantic drives down the old A4 to Kensington and a night of lost sleep.

'Frankie was meticulous about getting it right. I would find myself in his sitting-room in the early hours doing Frankie Howerd impressions to Frankie Howerd! I was trying to explain where the laugh was, and I'd be going: "No — what? Oh yes, missus . . ." while he sat opposite me solemnly writing it all down in a notebook. It was a weird experience.'

Over a glass (or two) of Scotch, David Hatch would patiently explain why he thought it was funny. Sometimes he would get a writer in to help.

'Frankie was difficult during rehearsals, no question about it. He would demand things you would never expect anyone to demand in a radio studio. Like the lighting had to be right! Now that's not something you normally expect of a radio programme, is it? But Frankie wanted to be sure that every person in that audience could see every flicker of his face, right back to the last row. If that meant fooling around with the lights, so be it.'

Frankie Howerd's moods were notorious — and totally unpredictable. The first anyone would know of it was when he arrived at the Paris Theatre with those limpet brows drawn close together in a thunderous scowl, and the bloodhound's face longer than ever.

'Frequently he was sullen and awkward,' Hatch recalls. 'It was a way of getting attention. He wanted everyone clamouring around him — everyone knew their job was to make the star *the star*. Nobody was allowed to take that away from him. That's what it was all about. And let's face it — he *was* the show.'

Just as notorious were Frankie's manic outbursts of temper — again based on his insecurity. 'He could be very rude, you'd hear him slagging off engineers or technicians, then saying sorry later. It was impossible to jolly him out of his bad moods. We just had to let him live through it. You could knock your brains out trying to cheer him up, but the only thing that worked was an audience laughing. Then the sun came out.'

The fraught hour immediately leading up to the show was the time all producers who worked with Frankie Howerd dreaded. 'That was when he started complaining. About the script, about the lights, about how he looked. He would get everyone jumpy and nervous, wondering if we'd ever be ready before the audience came in,' Hatch recalls.

'But that was all part of it. To create a climate of anxiety around him — he liked that. If he was worrying — why, so should everyone else. Then he was really happy! And when he had thoroughly worn us all to shreds, out he'd stroll on stage and have them all falling off their seats.'

From close quarters, Hatch observed the magic at work. 'Frankie had this tremendous rapport with the British public. They loved him. They could identify with that miserableness we all feel at some time, and there he was living it for them. "There but for the Grace of God . . ." They'd come in ready to laugh — and he never let them down.'

That laughter, cleansing unction to his self-doubts, flowed with Frankie's first words as he stepped up to the microphone and cast his eyes sombrely over the packed seats.

'*I'm feeling dismal tonight* . . . [Sympathetic cries of '*Aaah*' from the audience] . . . *That's right, get your aaahs out! Let's have all the big aaahs* . . . *It's sad, though* . . . *I'm feeling a bit* — *limp. Oh, you as well, sir?* . . . *Mine's a different reason* . . .'

Another successful show in the can. Frankie smiling and apologizing all round. 'You were right about the script,' he told David more than once. And: 'I shouldn't have made all that fuss, should I? I know I'm difficult.'

Thinking about it, counting the battle scars, Hatch's smile is a trifle tight. 'You always got the apology afterwards — but it didn't stop him doing it the next week . . .'

The time that Frankie over-stepped the mark once too often occurred on a Sunday after he had asked for a full day's 'trial run'. Hatch recalls: 'He wanted everyone there early. So I fixed it all up, and called the cast and crew in to be there by ten o'clock in the morning.' Everyone duly assembled, including June Whitfield and Ray Allen, the comedy 'feed'. David's wife Ann spent two hours preparing smoked salmon and ham sandwiches for a light buffet lunch and drove in from Hounslow with them.

One person didn't turn up. Frankie . . .

A stream of increasingly irate phone calls to his home produced no reply. Hatch was so livid he scribbled out a 'filthy note' on the spot, marched round to the Palladium where Frankie was appearing during the week, and left it at the stage door.

'I was outraged, really furious with him. He turned up finally in the afternoon, with no explanation, no apology. He was a very naughty boy. But he got my note — and wrote me a funny letter back: *You should be a writer . . . You know how to express such emotion.* I mean, what can you do with a man like that?'

If Frankie could be impossible at times, there were ways and means to get your way without him spotting it. But you needed to know the tricks of the trade. One who succeeded — though at a price, after surviving the initial overtures — was Richard Willcox, currently Deputy Head of Light Entertainment, an amiable and popular figure within the BBC.

In 1978, as a senior producer, he seemed the ideal choice to look after Frankie's new radio series, now extended to an hour and titled *The Frankie Howerd Variety Show*. Once again the Paris Theatre was the venue — only this time on a far grander scale. A 24-piece orchestra backed him up. Guest stars like Rosemary Squires and Norman Vaughan appeared. Frankie came on first with an early monologue to set the mood of fun and frivolity.

'*Ladies and gentle-men! . . .*' And straight into rudery. '*Now calm down. I've got to tell you this. I was having a bath, see . . . The thing was, I hadn't got any clothes on . . . ooh no . . . So there I was, lying there in the water . . . I looked down . . . you're right, missus, I noticed something! No listen* — lis-sen! *It was staring me in the face . . . Cor, we've got a right lot 'ere tonight! . . . A protruberance . . . I thought: you've got a big tummy . . .*'

Then he would introduce his guests, ending with a question–answer session with his fans. In fact, they were planted members of the BBC staff, primed to shout out silly questions. Every single question was scripted.

There were to be eight shows in all. Seasoned comedy writers Laurence Marks and Maurice Gran were joined by Jimmy Melville and Rory McGrath to add warmth, weight and wit to the 22-carat show that under Willcox's adroit hand had become a major production to rival any in the West End. 'It was a very expensive programme,' the producer remembers. But a flagship for BBC comedy, with huge ratings.

Half-way through, Richard Willcox dropped out. He was forced to take a short spell in hospital — suffering from nervous exhaustion. His place was taken by a raw young producer whose nerves were a-quiver on much the same wavelength as Frankie's — name of Griff Rhys-Jones.

Like them all, Willcox remembers his relationship with his temperamental star as the love—hate kind. Like David Hatch, he grew to dread Sundays, and never made any dinner dates on Saturday nights. But, recognizing a fellow professional, he is generous in his praise.

'Frankie's monologues were just wonderful. He was extraordinary, the most amazing man. Yet he was so unsure of himself that he couldn't make a rational judgement on a script. He needed our advice to get him through it.'

That, of course, led to delays and ructions. 'I'm ashamed to say we had to resort to an old trick when we brought him a script to approve — a script which he immediately threw out,' Willcox admits, but without any real shame.

It was in the weeks leading up to the actual first show, the creative period when the writers and producer hammer out ideas and words and finally offer them to the star, that he had to pull the wool over Frankie's baggy but eagle eyes.

Willcox had taken the script to the house in Edwardes Square. In the ground-floor morning-room where Frankie always talked business, the comic faced the producer, black eyebrows clinging together like a pair of limpets on heat.

'I don't like it,' he said tersely. 'Take it away and rewrite it!'

Richard sighed, obediently gathered up the offending script, and departed.

Three days later he was back. Two hours, two Scotches and a lot of raised voices after that, he was seeing himself out again — still with the script under his arm. 'In all I went back six times,' he recalls. 'The boys rewrote it and rewrote it until they were blue in the face. In the end they gave up.

'I went back at last with the *original* script, and said: "I think we've cracked it!" Frankie went through it, looked up, and said: "Now that's much better!" And a week later he went on stage and did it.

'The truth is that he had no idea of what was good and what was bad. And he relied totally on his writers.'

Willcox goes along with the theory about Frankie's increasingly mercurial moods, a premise that was voiced on more than one occasion in the BBC Club in Langham Place after a particularly noisy outburst from the star in petulant humour.

'If he got the mixture of pills and brandy wrong — watch out. He would be in the wrong mood for hours. But if he got it right, he'd be absolutely brilliant! I have never known a man swing from such huge highs to dreadful lows in a single afternoon. It was hard going for a producer.'

In the end, too hard for Richard Willcox, who finally succumbed to a dose of depressive 'Frankie-itis' and retired from the fray to have a few weeks off. He would later be promoted to Chief Producer, and then into the upper echelons of Light Entertainment. But he never forgot his days with Frankie.

The writers helped. They were young, and they were cheeky, and they pulled Frankie's leg to try to jolt him out of a bad mood. Frankie paid them back where it counted — in the decibel levels of laughter he earned for them for all the hours of agonizing and frustration.

'*I thought: I must do something about my physique. Physique, missus! . . . Diet! That was the answer . . . have you read about this cholesterol? . . . Oooh yes . . . People are getting too much of this cholesterol, and it's making them poorly . . . It beats me why they want to drink motor oil in the first place . . .*' That was one worthy of his old school magazine.

The last show in the series, and Frankie was in overdrive. He was backed by the Irish comic Pat Mooney, who came on strong with some splendid Oirish patter. Like the one about the burglar who wore white wellies so that he wouldn't leave tracks in the snow . . . or the labourer who walked into a Kilburn pub with a handful of horse manure in his hand, plonked it down on the counter and said: 'Look what I nearly stepped in!'

Closer to the knuckle, where he was most at home, Frankie in full flood was a sight to relish.

'*I went along to this restaurant in Hampstead . . . yes, very posh. It was called the Running Bean . . . Very select it was, where all the beautiful people go . . . All right, sir, there's always one, and it's always in the front row . . . 'Ere, but I thought I'd have soup of the day, so I ordered Cream of Wednesday . . . The food*

*was shocking. Gawd 'elp us! Nettle Hot Pot. Nut Rissoles — and
Cow Pat Roly-Poly . . . Oh yes — what? I've been grappling with
my nut cutlets . . . Oh, titter ye not . . .'*

Richard Willcox remembers a nightmarish broadcast, live from
Earls Court. It was a day he would prefer to forget. With his co-
producer, David Raven-Allen, he assembled various actors,
entertainers and musicians to commemorate some anniversary or
other — the Beeb is always having anniversaries.

But this one was b-i-g. What's more, it was going out live, to
an estimated audience of eleven million. *The Radio Show, Radio
Show* (weird title, but who's counting?) was mounted in the vast
expanse of the Earls Court exhibition centre, with a man-made
arena set up to accommodate selected shows.

Frankie was the star of his particular bill. The first tremors
raced through the production team when he arrived, looking more
rumpled than ever, and clutching a bottle of brandy in a brown
paper bag in one determined hand. A bag that he wouldn't let
go. Possibly to justify the title, Frankie was already seeing double
when his turn came to take the stage — and it showed.

He was due to be on for seven minutes. The all-important
schedules, worked out back in 'BH' with the precision of a military
operation down to the last second, had his act cut and dried. Even
a seven-second overlap was considered a cardinal sin.

Frankie over-ran by seven minutes, precisely double his allotted
time.

*'My diction . . . This man said my diction should be better . . .
Oooh the cheek of it . . . He said my vowels should be more open.
I resent that! There's nothing wrong with my vowels . . .'*

The audience howled, clamouring for more. Frankie, suffused
with triumph and brandy, forgot his script and obliged them. For
once he was genuinely adlibbing. 'He left his rehearsed patter and
reverted to old jokes.' Richard Willcox cringes at the memory.
Because Frankie lost them — the public that is. Standing on the
rostrum, looking down at his audience and the less-amused
members of the Corporation who had rumbled it and suddenly
didn't know where to look in embarrassment, he went off on a
rambling trail down a memory lane of tired jokes and dull tales
of woe.

'He over-ran, the whole programme over-ran, everything after that over-ran throughout the night,' the co-producer recalls. David Raven-Allen is one of the old school, an author who has written more than twenty books, and for four years in the mid eighties had been responsible for the long-running *Friday Night is Music Night*. To him, Frankie was a one-off, a wayward soul who had strayed off the straight and narrow and gone his own way, with dire results.

In short, that night Frankie blew it.

'I just wish we had had a hook to pull him off,' says Raven-Allen. 'But there was no way of getting him to go.' The red light glowed, they stayed on air. Francis was hooked on brandy, uppers, and the euphoria of the occasion.

Afterwards he said: 'Wasn't that great!'

And fumbled in his brown paper bag.

The TV series that kept Frankie at the top in the seventies and early eighties was *Up Pompeii*. Frankie would tell friends later that the idea came from two unnamed BBC executives who were in Pompeii. 'They said: "Let's do something about this place – apart from rebuilding it." ' Whatever the source, Frankie took his toga out of the wardrobe and became Lurcio the slave, beckoning the audience into his confidence with a leering intimacy that proved too much for more sensitive ears – although out of twelve million viewers, only a handful actually rang the BBC switchboard to complain.

Mary Whitehouse called it 'sordid and cheap'. Frankie called it vulgar – 'And I've never known anyone who was corrupted by vulgarity,' he said, not for the first time in his life. 'In a way it's comforting, in the best traditions of the British music hall, with the comic wearing a toga.'

For openers Frankie would set the tone without any preamble, so that at least viewers were aware they had not tuned in to *Open University*. '*I'm not the Major Domo,*' he explained. Pause. Then: '*I said Domo, and let's 'ave no misunderstanding at the commencement –*'

The steps of the Forum were peopled by slave girls and a range of outrageous characters such as Ludicrous Sextus the Senator, his wife Ammonia, his son Nausius and his daughter Erotica. 'So delightfully chaste,' said an admirer. '*And so easily caught up with!*' muttered Lurcio darkly.

As the ratings rose, so at last did Frankie's spirits. He worked incessantly at polishing every grimace and nuance, rehearsing every pause, every panicky glance over the shoulder, as well as the mock indignation and outrage.

'After all, *Up Pompeii* is only an interrupted patter act, that's the way I see it,' he reasoned. Indeed, the whole show was built around him. 'I give ideas, but I don't write the scripts. Other writers are so much better than I am.

'But I plan routines and photograph them mentally, like chapters in a book. The reason I don't adlib often is because I'm not very good at it. You don't adlib a Grieg piano concerto, do you? Or a gourmet meal? You plan them.

'If I can claim to be an actor at all, it's because I give the impression of being spontaneous.'

Frankie moved house once more. This time to a tall, narrow terraced house in a corner of leafy Edwardes Square, Kensington. Outside, a small area of crazy paving was relieved only by a large urn. The inside had a comfortable untidiness, not unlike its owner, apart from the living-room which was a study in elegance. Red Persian carpets, handsome flock wallpaper, inlaid antique table, deep settees. The overall effect was one of unostentatious good taste.

The glass shelves were crowded with Frankie's awards: the Variety Club Silver Heart for the 1968 Show Business Personality of the Year . . . the Water Rats award . . . a silver cigarette box from Lord Delfont for 'the man who never missed a show' after the 408 performances of *Way Out in Piccadilly* . . . plus a mounted truncheon from the men of 'A' Division CID, to commemorate one of his many shows for the police throughout the country . . .

On 2 March 1977 Frankie Howerd was awarded the OBE in the New Year's honours list, and dutifully donned top hat and morning suit to receive his gong from the Queen Mum. The last time he had set foot inside Buckingham Palace had been twenty-seven years before, when he entertained the staff at a Christmas concert. He told the Queen Mother: 'I never thought I would be

coming back for this honour.' Genuinely moved, his eyes filled
with tears as he faced the cameras afterwards. But he still managed
to quip: 'Apart from knocking over two footmen, it all went
smoothly.'

Another TV series, *Whoops Baghdad* for the BBC, kept the
fun rolling along. Same jokes, different background. For Lurcio,
read Ali Oopla, the Jeeves of the Grand Wazir (played by Derek
Francis), whose over-sexed daughter (Anna Brett) rejoiced in the
name of Boobiana.

Cue for Frankie to eye her with the comment: *'So this is what
is known as a booby trap. Oooh . . . aaah . . . Like the sands
of the desert, she never grows cold. You know what they call 'er
round here? "New potatoes". 'Cos she's always in the sack.'*

It was in the eighties that Frankie faced yet another crisis in his
career. Work was coming in. A TV show here, a pantomime there.
But somehow the sparkle had faded. Alas, poor Francis! We knew
him well . . . But now he was compelled to forego the bright lights
of the West End that had once shone so vividly on him, and go
out into clubland once again.

First stop: a short season at one of London's sophisticated
'mushroom clubs', the Country Cousin in Fulham. Patrons
arrived to find notices all over the foyer: 'Frankie Howerd —
Brilliant! Scintillating wit!' He walked out in front of the tables
and launched into a passionate tirade against the club owner. *'I
mean, the embarrassment of it, no, really . . . What am I going
to do? . . . I don't know where to look . . . No . . . honest, I
really don't . . .'*

'People really believed he had put them up. He hadn't, of
course. They were props. It was an idea I thought up the week
before, and it worked.'

Behind his decision was a battle to overcome yet another
personal and professional crisis. 'The hurtful truth was that I was
afraid I had lost my nerve,' he confessed in an interview. 'I had
been offered the London Palladium — and I turned it down. I
made the excuse that I was too busy. But beneath the bravado
I was scared. So I went for the soft option, and played it safe.'

The soft option took him to Singapore for a one-night stint
in a club, to a commercial in the Alps, to a business convention

in Venice. The money came in, but his self-esteem took another battering. Finally he faced up to his fear — and took on the trendy Country Cousin audiences.

They loved him. The old Frankie was back — even if, like Maurice Chevalier, he had his farewell speech prepared 'in case it all fell apart'.

13

In The Wars

Frankie Howerd was modest to the point of invisibility when it
came to heroism. If he fought World War II from way inside our
own lines, it was probably the safest place not just for him but
for our boys, too. If anyone was going to shoot himself in the
foot, it was Bombardier Howard F.A. − and who knew how
many he would have brought down with him?

But there was no doubting his moral and physical courage, even
if he would have been the most reluctant soldier in the field.
Witness the events of other wars, when he went quietly, if not
fearlessly into the front lines. But then the definition of a hero
has always been someone who knows he's afraid, admits it −
and still has the courage to do the job he's given. Frankie never
pretended he wasn't anything but scared witless, and never
considered himself particularly brave.

But in Northern Ireland, bullets pinged off the armoured cars
in which he huddled. He ran the gauntlet of stones and Molotov
cocktails bursting around his small but determined troupe. In
Borneo, a tribe of headhunters sized up his hat measurements
from the trees. And in Cyprus, anti-British EOKA terrorists were
in the crowd when he performed in Nicosia.

That takes guts.

Particularly when you have a phobia about flying . . .

But Frankie was determined that the show should go on. The
thin brown or blue line keeping what was left of the British
Presence intact overseas needed its transfusion of laughter. If there
was a trouble spot, he wanted to be in it. Bobby Jaye, a senior
BBC figure and an ex-Cavalry officer himself, was Head of Light
Entertainment when the Falklands War became reality in 1984.
The armada was scarcely out of the Solent before the direct line
to his first-floor office in Langham Place rang − and Frankie's
voice came through. Sober, slow-spoken, deliberate.

'I want to get down to the Falklands,' he said. 'As soon as
possible. I know you can arrange it.'

In fact it would have taken rather more than pressing a button to have Frankie Howerd in the thick of the action. Bobby, knowing his man well, stalled for time. 'I'll have to try and find someone to go with you,' he said. 'It won't be easy.'

Frankie turned to another possible source for his ticket south. Derek Agutter was a wartime major who had become head of CSE (Combined Services Entertainment) in 1965, finally retiring at sixty in 1985 after twenty years of fun and games escorting his stars into the world's hot spots. Tommy Cooper, Matt Monroe, Frankie Vaughan, Dickie Henderson and Harry Secombe are just some of the stars who gave their time and their talent willingly as morale boosters to the troops stationed anywhere from Aden to Armagh, or from Borneo to Belize.

Frankie had become a regular on the team, a foot soldier slogging through desert or jungle to reach the far-flung outposts of the small red patches on the world map that were the remnants of the British Empire. The old forces entertainment of ENSA – known to all ranks as 'Every Night Something Awful' – had been taken over by CSE ('Chaos Succeeds Ensa') which is based in Chalfont St Giles, Buckinghamshire.

That was where the phone rang in the boss's office. Major Agutter (father of actress Jenny, the teenage star of *The Railway Children* and never allowed by the Press to forget it) answered. Frankie again.

'He was mad keen to go, and really most insistent,' recalls Major Agutter. 'But there was no way we were going to put him into a C130 Hercules for a nonstop twenty-six hour flight into a war zone. His age, for one thing. And he had a bad knee, too, which was constantly troubling him. I managed to dissuade him, but he was very upset – as only Frankie could be.'

Major Agutter had seen Frankie upset before, but only when a spotlight didn't work, or the script didn't sound right. Or when he was flying – 'In Cyprus in 1974 we took a helicopter up to the Troudos mountains, one of the most spectacular vistas in the world. I pointed down, and said: "Look at that view, Frankie. Isn't it simply magnificent?"

'But his eyes were screwed tight shut in sheer terror, and he refused to open them the whole flight! The poor chap had a phobia about flying – though he still went out with us anywhere if we asked him.' That day Frankie opened them long enough to go on the air for a live linked-up broadcast with the Jimmy Young 'Prog' back in Broadcasting House.

In real danger, Frankie kept his eyes wide open all the time — and his head down as instructed — but never raised a murmur of protest.

In 1974 the Turks had invaded Cyprus. The British bases were on alert, wives and girlfriends had been evacuated home. 'The lads were extremely browned-off,' Frankie recalled. When CSE rang to ask for his services, he responded with alacrity, and on 2 September flew out with singer Lois Lane, the singing trio of Elaine, Joy and Ray Avon, and blonde actress Julie Ege to add a spot of glamour.

They did six shows in four days, from a sports field in Dekhelia in front of 1,500 men, mainly from the 9th Signal Regiment, to the open Curium Amphitheatre with 2,000 troops squatting on the great circular stone steppes above the stage. Frankie's mind went back first to *Up Pompeii* — then eighteen years further back to recall how he had last performed in that same arena. That was when the dangerous EOKA terrorists were shooting British servicemen in the streets of Nicosia — and morale-boosting support from back home was also regarded as a prime target for terror.

'You feel very vulnerable, stuck out in the open,' he admitted later. 'I couldn't wait to scuttle off.' But if he was scared, no one had a hint of it.

Not that day, nor others. Writer Peter Evans followed Frankie and his stalwart team into the steaming jungles of Borneo in August 1965 to see the effect on the troops at first-hand. 'FRONT-LINE FRANKIE' blared the headline — and it wasn't far off. Nor was Frankie far off from the skirmishing, the sniping and the ambush that was the pattern of the war against Communist insurgents.

As their RAF helicopter flew low over the green carpet of trees, Evans overheard Frankie confess to the pilot, 'To be honest, I'm terrified.'

Came the reassuring reply: 'You only die once, sir!'

To which Frankie responded sombrely: 'Look, you have to

understand I'm a coward, and this must be taken into account when you make a statement like that!'

With the Australian zither player Shirley Abicair, singer Mary Murphy, and a magician who called himself Koran in support, Frankie had flown out in an RAF Comet via Gan, the tiny RAF staging-post in the Indian Ocean, where they had given their first show. On to Singapore, for two more shows. Then a long drive of one-night stands all the way to Kuala Lumpur.

In Singapore they were met off the plane by a young Lieutenant, Adam Rassim, complete with crisp moustache and a cane under one arm. In the coach he ran through a schedule that looked as if it would take up twenty-five hours a day and leave them no time to eat or sleep. Frankie didn't like it one bit. To him it sounded more like the briefing he'd had for his first route march back in basic training in the war.

'What's your rank?' he demanded.

'Lieutenant, sir.'

'Well,' said Frankie, lying to his back teeth. 'I'm a General. So listen carefully.' For once he didn't say *lis-sen*. 'You seem to have us in a dozen places at once all the time we're on the tour. We'll do our best, because we don't want to disappoint the lads. But remember we're not a bunch of buskers — and we haven't been paid to come out here. Understood?'

'Yes — sir!'

'Good,' barked Frankie. 'Any questions?'

'Er — just one. Are you prepared to visit the forward fighting areas when we get to Borneo?'

'*They'd* be delighted,' responded Frankie, keeping a straight face.

'Good show,' said the officer, much relieved.

Frankie relented. 'You're in show business now,' he said. 'It's tough — not like the Army!'

He always started his act the same way. '*This is all a terrible mistake,*' he'd tell them, his lugubrious countenance turning this way and that like an old bloodhound sniffing the air. '*This colonel chap at the War Office started it, see. He asked me whether I wanted to go to Borners. Well, I thought he meant Bournemouth, so I said yes. And here I am — now don't laugh! It's not funny —*'

But it was, and they did. And their spirits were lifted for two precious hours when they could forget the mosquitoes and the wet-sauna heat, and the lurking danger of a sniper's bullet or a booby-trap mine.

And Frankie Howerd had won himself literally an army of fans, who would talk for months on end about the night they saw him on a makeshift stage in a jungle clearing in the middle of nowhere, and be his friends for life.

Up country in the front line of Tepoi, no more than three thousand measured yards from the Indonesian border, Frankie was greeted by the Commander of 19 Brigade, Sir David Fraser, and by another fresh-faced young lieutenant, Neil Carlier, who was seconded to look after him. Carlier, ex-Highgate School and Sandhurst, would later rise in the ranks to become Commander-in-Chief of the Falklands for the first two important years after the war.

He recalls: 'Frankie was a giggle a minute. He did marvels for the morale of the troops. He never complained about the heat or the flies, but just got on with the job — of being the funniest man we'd seen there. He only had to open his mouth, and we all fell about.'

Frankie arrived at the front line by the now infamous chopper. Too many had fallen out of the sky for comfort, mainly through malfunctioning of their equipment. Even the nuts and bolts didn't feel safe. No one dared to tell their star guest. So Frankie beamed down in blissful ignorance of the dangers, and despite a swollen ankle after tripping on a rock, he kept going in the sweltering heat for the four scheduled days, constantly pouring sweat in one hundred per cent humidity that ensured he would lose at least half a stone in weight. Which he duly did.

They put him into one of the Long Houses that formed 19 Brigade's makeshift encampment — a rattan and bamboo house on stilts above the fetid marshes. Beneath the sagging floor unidentifiable creatures swam in the murky river below, and the troops had been warned not to set foot in the water, let alone swim there. The lads called the houses 'Sticks and strings on stilts'. All they contained was a thin mattress with a single cotton blanket over it, a cupboard to hang one's clothes in — and a hole in the floor in one corner.

'What's that for?' Frankie inquired with interest, peering down through the hole into the weed-infested marsh ten feet beneath.

'We call it a loo,' Carlier told him in some embarrassment. 'Sorry, but that's all there is – '

'Don't worry,' said Frankie, who for once knew better than to argue. 'I'll get by.'

Frankie would tell the story back home – after downing beer with the boys in the ramshackle bar following the performance, next morning's sound effects were 'Oooh . . . aaah . . . splosh!'

Frankie under fire was a sight to behold. His first trip into a war zone had been to Korea in 1952. After that came regular forays. he had braved insurgents in the North Arab protectorates in the sixties, done a Navy Lark gig on the Ark Royal moored off Aden, scorned the EOKA shoot-in-the-back gunmen in Cyprus.

Northern Ireland though, that was something else.

All his trips to Belfast were top secret, revealed to the Press and its readers only on the day after Frankie and his courageous troubadours had left. But in the past twenty years of 'the Troubles' he had survived shootings, bomb explosions, and – oddly enough the act which personally affected his most – the nightmare of having stones and flaming Molotov cocktails hurled at him by shouting crowds of youths, venting their hatred on the British Army and anyone who supported it.

The 'Tour', as it was euphemistically described, was always made up of ten artistes: Frankie, aided and abetted by a three-piece group (piano, bass guitar, drums), a girl singer, a speciality act, a comic, and three leggy dancers. For once Frankie was on his own, minus the indefatigable Madame Blanche or Miss Rogers at the piano.

The 'spesh' act was the 'Mighty Mannequin' – otherwise Joan Rhodes, a beautiful, leggy blonde who tore up telephone books and bent steel bars in her teeth as 'the world's strongest woman'. In the Belfast barracks on one tour, Joan was presented with a rubber bullet after her act by admiring troops of 45 Commando Royal Marines – only to find Frankie peering over her shoulder and demanding: 'Hey, what about one for me?'

'He was really insistent,' says Joan. 'Though I can't possibly think what he was going to do with it.'

Frankie was a-mazed by Joan's muscles – and the femininity

that went with them, an integral part of an international act which had attracted both red-blooded males and a gay following alike. King Farouk once offered her £1,000 to go to bed with him, an offer Joan demurely declined.

Frankie offered no more than open-mouthed admiration. When she invited him to try to tear a telephone book in half or bend one of her nails, he blanched theatrically and said: 'Oooh no, darling. But I might just paint them for you.'

The banter disguised long hours of tension in a potentially deadly situation. Each tour normally took no more than four days, but to those unused to being under combat alert, it seemed a lifetime. Major Agutter recalls: 'Frankie was terrific. He always wanted to go wherever the troops were serving in the most dangerous places, knowing they would be without their families, on their own and in real trouble spots. He had no regard for his own safety. I had to insist on going along to look after him.'

Frankie found himself in border barracks that had come under fire from the IRA, in places written in blood like Crossmaglen, South Armagh, Derry, even in the Maze prison where he gave a show to the warders – but not to the prisoners. On more than one trip across the beleaguered province he came under attack – 'But it wasn't personally directed at the performers, purely at the Army,' assures Major Agutter, remembering the tense days on the road.

'We travelled in "pigs", the armoured cars we felt we had to put them in for their own safety. I said to Frankie: "Don't worry if you hear a bang, or feel the impact of something hitting the side. It won't get through." They were stones and petrol bombs, and more than once we had a lot of trouble getting past. But we always made it.'

The worst day Frankie experienced was the show he was due to give in the Flax Mill off the notorious Falls Road area of Belfast. It was in one of what his hosts were calling, with admirable understatement, 'a rather sticky period'. Frankie found out what that meant when he set off with his troupe in a fleet of armoured cars to the converted cotton mill where the lads of 2nd Battalion, Royal Green Jackets, were waiting. 'The first clang on the roof made me jump,' he said much later, safe back in mainland Britain. 'We couldn't see a blind thing, but we heard all the missiles raining down. Talk about sweat — it was pouring off me before I even saw the audience!'

Frankie also heard the whine of a sniper's bullet more than once, but played down any notion that he was in real danger. Of course, he was. But he never let that fear show. If he was all a-quiver, it was down to his usual nerves about stepping out on to a stage, and those just couldn't be helped.

To the distant crump of explosions, he started off by telling them about the London taxi-driver taking a fare to Heathrow for a flight to Belfast, who asked him: 'This man's father is my father's son. Who is it?'

The Irishman in the back said: 'Oi give up.'

'It's me,' said the cabbie.

The Irishman repeated the joke to a friend in a Belfast pub. 'Who is it?' he asked.

'Sure it's yerself,' said the friend.

'No, it's not,' said the other. 'It's a taxi-driver over in London!'

As a last gesture Frankie always gave any fee away to an Army charity. The Ulster branch of the Royal Artillery Association benefited more than once from his generosity.

Frankie gave vent to his true feelings when he turned up without warning at Major (now plain Mister) Agutter's farewell party at the CSE Headquarters in Chalfont St Giles, and with no persuasion at all made an impromptu speech — something he normally detested.

'I could never make up my mind whether you were mad, foolhardy or courageous every time you went to Northern Ireland,' he told the retiring officer. 'I think it must have been all three.'

'Don't you mean "we", Frank?' observed Mr Agutter, returning what was undoubtedly a heartfelt compliment.

14
Fond Farewell

Frankie Howerd always protested that he was no good at after-dinner speeches. In fact, Francis protesteth too much. All he had to do was get to his feet — but that, of course, was the hard part. Not because of any over-indulgence of alcohol, Frankie seldom fell into that trap in public — it was just sheer nerves.

But the moment that jolted him out of the rut for his final extraordinary comeback came when he least expected it. In fact, it was simply a chance remark. But those few words put Frankie back in the front line again, bringing him a whole new following.

The eighties had seen him casting around for an audience, dangerously close to losing the identity he had built up over so many painstaking years. He had narrated a TV children's series for Central. He had tried his hand at a spot of Gilbert and Sullivan, as Sir Joseph Porter in *HMS Pinafore*. He had been a guest on TV shows ranging from 3—2—1 to Wogan to Roland Rat. He had been out on the road as a roving reporter for TV-am. He even gave his name to a board game called *Orgy*.

That fickle finger had been dormant for too long. Now it had him in its sights again. When it came to physical accidents, Frankie was in a class of his own. He slipped on a patch of ice in Birmingham and cracked a bone in his back. He fell again and hurt his knee so badly he had to have an operation in 1987 that effectively put him out of action for six months. He even overbalanced and plummeted over a balcony while on holiday in the Canary Islands, and was lucky to escape with no more than a few bruises.

As Goldfinger once remarked to James Bond at a critical moment: 'Once is coincidence, twice is happenstance, three times is enemy action!' When it came to looking after himself, poor Frankie was his own worst enemy.

But suddenly the tide turned. And it can be traced back to the evening of 16 April 1989 in the ballroom of the Marriott Hotel in Mayfair.

One of Frankie's regular dates was with the Gallery First Nighters' Club, a splendidly eccentric group of theatre-going faithfuls who, as their name indicates, queue religiously for hours on end for a seat in the gods at every new play or show in town.

They hold one major dinner a year, usually in April, plus a smaller one in a second month, which is a flexible date. There is always a guest of honour, sometimes two − as in the case of Michael Denison and Dulcie Gray, a husband and wife stage team who seemed destined to endure for ever.

Dulcie published her autobiography *Looking Forward, Looking Back* in 1991, and mentioned the Gallery First Nighters' dinner in 1989 where she and Michael were the guests, and Frankie was chief speaker. As far as Dulcie was concerned, he was marvellous − funny, witty, affectionately insulting, typical Francis in overdrive.

What she didn't know was what it took to get Frankie to his feet. Sitting on the top table two seats away from Jack Rossiter, the club's president of twenty-three years, the comedian suddenly found his legs had gone.

Mr Rossiter noticed his guest speaker was trembling. He leaned across anxiously.

'Are you all right?'

'I − I'm not sure −' Frankie's words came hesitantly. He looked as if he were about to get up and run from the room in the direction of the nearest cloakroom, lock himself in, and stay there.

'Yes you are,' said Mr Rossiter firmly. In his seventy-nine years he had seen more cases of stage fright than anyone else in the room. He gave Frankie a fierce glare. '*It's just another show − all right?*'

There was a long pause. Then: 'All right,' Frankie responded meekly. And repeated: 'Just another show . . .'

The gavel of toastmaster Ivor Spencer smacked down to bring the banqueting room to silence. And after a spirited introduction from Jack Rossiter, Frankie was up, up and away.

'He was marvellous that night,' Mr Rossiter recalls. 'He just grabbed us from the moment he stood up and never let go.'

Three hundred people stood and applauded at the end, as a sweating Frankie mopped his brow, bestowed a wicked wink on

Dulcie, and slumped back in his seat. Dulcie would pen in her memoirs, on page 173, 'Frankie gave one of the best speeches I had ever heard.'

No one told her how it nearly didn't happen.

Afterwards Frankie shook Mr Rossiter's hand and said: 'What you said back there – '

'Yes – ?'

'It's what I wanted to hear.' That was all he said. But from that moment, there was a new lease of life to Frankie's performances – and it paid off. *Just another show.*

He started speaking at private business functions and government institutions. He gave a lecture on the art of comedy to students at Cambridge, and turned it into a riotous assembly. He embarked on a one-man show with twenty-five venues around the country and packed them out from a fringe theatre in Wakefield to the Golden Garter at Wythenshawe.

But now his audiences were different. New, young, trendy, the kind they call in show business parlance 'off the wall'. The torn jeans brigade queued to see him. When Sid Vicious announced that Frankie was his main man, Francis found himself being clapped through the throng by bands of punk rockers.

'*What do you mean, you thought I was dead?*' he shouted at them, and they roared back their acclaim. He flapped a protesting hand. '*Nay, nay, and thrice times nay!*'

Fringe theatre meant the Albany Empire in the East End, where the audience was practically squatting at his feet. Frankie, full of new-found confidence thanks to his modern army of supporters, would camp it up by coming on the tiny stage in his brown suit – with a glittering diamanté purse over one wrist. '*I wasn't going to leave THAT in the dressing-room. Well, I mean, would you?*' He came on aggressively, forearms bursting from his cuffs, socks subsiding down to his ankles, his shirt flapping open at the navel. The eyebrows seemed to be intensified into fresh thickets of innuendo and the blue eyes were almost mesmeric as he took in the roomful of devout new disciples.

He called them his Frankie Pankies and had T-shirts made with the slogan *Get Your Titters Out* emblazoned on the front.

Frankie's last 'legit' West End success was his one-man show at the Garrick in May 1990, where it had transferred from the

Lyric, Hammersmith. In attendance was 'Madame Sunny Rogers at the Piano'. The show was a sell-out, and the critics loved it too.

It was a short run − 'for three weeks only' − but a merry one. It drew celebrities like bees to honey and the atmosphere was a nightly tonic both to Frankie and to his audiences. One old flame (in a strictly platonic sense) who came to applaud was Barbara Windsor. She still laughs at how Frankie greeted her backstage afterwards.

'He poured out the gin-and-tonics, raised his glass, and said: "Can you believe I'm still doing the same old rubbish I've been doing for years?" But a whole new generation of young people had discovered him − and they loved him. I think he was stunned by the new adulation . . . but he wasn't complaining. Not one bit.'

The climax of that year of living dangerously was Frankie's celebrated appearance before the Oxford Union in November 1990. The hour-long assault on tomorrow's intelligentsia was televized, and repeated as a tribute after his death. Frankie had them laughing from the start − *'You'll have to believe me when I say I'm not an intellectual . . .'* he began.

A voice from the back shouted: 'Here, here!'

'. . . which is why I feel so at home here tonight,' Frankie shot back.

The event was recorded for posterity. Or posterior, seeing that a sketch about a vicar addressing a nudist conference ended with Frankie baring his cheeks in a startling rearguard action as he made for the exit. It was generally agreed to be a bad taste finale, but it is doubtful if Frankie gave it a second thought. He was too busy thanking his lucky stars for another chance to shine.

Frankie took his stars seriously. From his early days within the Church's embrace he had been obsessed by life, death and the hereafter. Following the death of his mother he found solace in the person of psychic healer Doris Collins, and would visit her at her home in Richmond for comfort and advice. 'He adored his mum,' said Doris. 'He would sit with me, and she would come through and talk about his problems. It gave him a great deal of comfort.'

Two months after his death Frankie 'appeared' to the medium during a seminar she was conducting with fifty students in the

Arthur Findlay College, Stanstead. Frankie, it seems, was in typically acerbic form. 'I saw his face and heard his voice,' Miss Collins asserts firmly. 'He looked around and said crossly: "Who are all these bloody people?" He didn't want anyone around when he talked to me, he made that very plain. He said he'd come back later.'

Max Bygraves knew of Frankie's fascination with the occult, and particularly with the hereafter. He had watched it grow from a hobby into a passion, particularly as the years started to race by. 'He was into reading palms and tea leaves, ever since I first knew him,' Max says, looking back to the early days when they were two penniless young comics hoping for the big break. 'We were in digs in Sheffield struggling to make fifteen quid a week. One morning over breakfast Frankie peered into my tea cup. Then he traced the lines on my hand, and said: "One day you'll be a millionaire." He was very serious.

' "Oh yeah?" I said. "That'll be the day!"

' "You will," he assured me. "Just you wait and see." '

The last time Max saw Frankie was a few weeks before he died. They had lunch together in Kensington, and Max inquired: 'Do you still read palms?'

Frankie nodded.

'And do you remember what you said to me all those years ago?'

'I do,' said Frankie. 'And I was right, wasn't I?' He gave his quirkish grin. 'So – you pay the bill! OK?'

'OK,' said Max. And paid.

For a member of such a notoriously vulnerable profession, and one with a deep interest in mysticism and the esoteric, Frankie exhibited a marked lack of superstition. While Norman Wisdom, for instance, kisses the wall of his dressing-room after a good week, and murmurs his thanks to whoever is watching over him, Frankie relied on the occasional prayer to see him through. He would drop into a church on the spur of the moment, and sit quietly by himself pondering on life, death and what might follow.

Except for one little foible. When Sunny Rogers told him how she always put her right shoe on first ever since her brother Ken assured her that it brought good luck, Frankie did the same.

Maybe he had two left feet, but it didn't always work.

As his self-doubts increased, so did the greatest doubt of all: his view of the Almighty. Long into the night at his corner table in the Al Gallo d'Oro, or later still after walking home to Edwardes Square, Frankie would agonize with friends over religion. 'How can God be benign when there's so much suffering in the world?' he would wonder aloud. 'Is He really responsible for everything that happens?' As the doctrine of creation changed with every new discovery in the cosmos, from biological evolution to the DNA chain, so Frankie was forced to try to persuade his old beliefs to come to terms with the new spiritual freedom he saw all around him.

He heard a lecture once, where a theologian declared: 'If God has the ability to intervene in something terrible about to happen, and does not − what then? How can you respect anyone who stands back, whether it be a parent or the great Father figure?' Looking around at the sorrows of the world, seeing for himself the violence and hatred in areas as far apart as the Borneo jungle and the urban jungle of Belfast, Frankie felt his soul troubled more than ever before.

Jeanne Mockford, herself a Catholic, recalls the perpetual debates. 'We used to have endless fierce arguments about religion. Over the years something was gnawing at him. When I first met Frankie, he had a Bible by his bedside. But not at the end. The Bible had gone. He just turned away from it.

'He went to his Maker as a non-believer, but as someone desperately *wanting* to believe.

'You couldn't change Frankie at any time, about anything. He had total tunnel vision. He had to work it out himself.'

Frankie gave a public clue to his heart-searching back in December 1965, when he was asked if he was religious. He replied: 'I was, yes.' then, after a pause: 'Why did I say "was"?'

Finally Frankie slid open a drawer, and put the Bible away. It had been on his bedside table all his life, the symbol of his unquestioning faith. But when the questions came, the answers didn't measure up. Frankie died an agnostic, though he was given a Christian burial.

One person, at least, is sure of Frankie's place in heaven. Dora Bryan is a devout Christian, a believer pure and simple in the Gospel, ignoring the trappings of theology or the complex whirlpools of philosophy. 'Frankie took three days to get to heaven. That's how long it took Jesus, isn't it?' she says, with total conviction.

'I always told him that's where he would end up, but in the end I'm not sure he believed me. When I heard he had died, I said a prayer for him. And I know in my heart he is there. And I am quite sure he is happy at last.'

Frankie would be sorely missed by the Royal Family. The Queen was amused by him, Prince Philip in particular roared with laughter at his innuendoes, and the Queen Mother thought him 'adorable'. He was her particular pet.

Lord Delfont tells a story of how he was invited to Windsor Castle to take tea and canapés with the Queen Mum in a small and intimate gathering following the 1968 Royal Variety Show. The afternoon turned into tea and sympathy for Francis when she suddenly said: 'Isn't it a shame about Frankie?'

'I'm sorry, ma'am?' For once Delfont was at a loss. What on earth was she talking about?

'His show in America. It's failed, you know. He was so wrong to try it. But I'm glad to see that at least the critics were kind to him.'

With the benefit of hindsight, Delfont can agree: 'It wasn't a good show for him. But he was desperate to prove himself as an actor as well as a comedian.'

The last time Delfont saw Frankie was when the comic appeared out of the blue at the Prince of Wales Theatre, to help celebrate the launch of Bernie's autobiography *East End, West End*. 'It was a marvellous gesture. We'd had a wonderful rapport, and I look back on him as a great loss to the theatre and to the world of comedy.

'He had an enormous inferiority complex. He doubted himself — but so has every comedian I've ever known. To me, being a stand-up comic is the hardest act in the world. If you go out there on your own, standing alone to keep an audience for an hour — it's a marvellous feat. And Frankie *could* do it.

'To me, he was one of the easiest artistes I ever worked with — and believe me, I've had some tough ones in my time. He never let me down in all the years I knew him.'

For Delfont, Frankie would remain a loner. 'He always seemed to be alone, mooching around by himself. But he had the most extraordinary career of any comedian − and the great thing is that with all the ups and downs, Frankie finished on top. What more could he have wished?'

One British entertainer who did make it in the US was Jim Dale, so much so that he now lives in New York. In the summer of 1992 he was invited by Peter Rogers to star in the title role of *Carry On Columbus* at Pinewood, and on location at Frensham Ponds (doubling for the Spanish Main). It was an offer Jim was happy to accept. He was a stalwart with the team, a veteran of several films, and invariably played the lusty hero. Even if he did lose his trousers as often as any of them.

Jim was particularly looking forward to seeing Frankie again. At the age of eighteen, as an up-and-coming young comic, they had shared the same agent. Stanley Dale also represented Eric Sykes, Spike Milligan, Ray Galton and Alan Simpson.

'I did a couple of shows at Army camps in England, doing the warm-up for Frankie. Can you believe that? I mean, warming the audience up for Frankie Howerd! I wouldn't say it was a difficult job − they just wanted me off! I got the biggest cheer when I left the stage!'

When he was filming *Sergeant Pepper* Frankie took an evening off to see Jim in a production of *The Comedians* at the Forum Theatre in Los Angeles. 'He came backstage during the intermission. I said: "Why don't I introduce you to the audience afterwards, and perhaps you can have a little chat with them." And that's what he did.

'Ironically the play is all about comics striving to make a living. I introduced Frankie, and bless his heart he went out there in front of a very cold audience who really didn't know him. And he was full of the "Oooh, hullo, Missus − I was a-mazed!" All that, in front of an absolute alien audience!

'He invited questions − and of course it's very difficult to ask questions of someone when you have no idea who he is or what he does! But Frankie won them over by saying: "I know another question you're simply aching to ask" − and then answering it himself! It takes a lot of nerve to do that.

'Afterwards we went out for a meal together and I just sat back and listened to him while he reminisced about the "good old days" – whenever they were!

'When I heard he had died I was absolutely shattered. I had several scenes with the King of Spain, and I had been rehearsing them with him in my mind's eye, visualizing his face and manner – until I got here and found he couldn't be in the show . . .'

Frankie left a brief legacy in the shape of a six-part series called *Frankie's On . . .* which would embrace Frankie doing his act before sailors on the *Ark Royal*, coal miners at Cotgrave Colliery, Nottingham, and doctors and nurses in hospital. Sadly, he only finished four before going into intensive care. The final two were never completed.

The *Ark Royal* episode contained several gems, vintage Frankie. '*The Captain said: "Are you H-o-w-d?"* ' He pronounced it '*Hard*', of course. '*I said: "No, not at the moment, and I haven't been for some time." Oooh, mocking Francis, they know how to hurt . . .*' And when heckled from the ranks, he fired his broadside: '*Why don't you join hands and try to contact the living!*' And to the coalminers: '*Get back to your shaft!*'

When Frankie went into the Harley Street Clinic with respiratory trouble in April 1992, none of his friends worried too greatly. He seemed to have been in and out of hospitals or consulting-rooms all his life, and always emerged with a smile and a quip.

But then the news broke: he was in intensive care, wired up to a heart machine. Daily bulletins described him as 'comfortable, but seriously ill'. In February he had been admitted to another hospital with a virus he had contracted on a trip to South America the previous year, but after treatment was pronounced 'all clear' and discharged. But in March he was back, this time in the Royal Nuffield Hospital for more tests.

The Harley Street Clinic became the focus of media attention. The pavement opposite the main entrance in Weymouth Street was crowded with photographers, as well as fans of Frankie who kept a day and night vigil. Ominously, even friends like Alfred Marks and Barbara Windsor were turned away. In his £1,000-a-day private room, with the curtains drawn, Frankie lay battling for his life.

The next day — a slight improvement. Messages of goodwill poured in from all over the country. Among them, one from Lord Delfont: 'I'm very sorry to hear of your illness, but delighted to know you're making jolly good progress. Please get well soon, as I'm thinking of doing a revival of *Ta-Ra-Ra-Boom-De-Ay!* — Affectionately, Berney' (Delfont's own spelling of his name).

Benny Hill, who with dreadful coincidence would die on the same day, Easter Sunday 19 April, sent a note: 'Stop trying to steal my act. I do the heart jokes.'

Sister Betty, along with Dennis Heymer, June Whitfield, Tessa Le Bars and Cilla Black, were allowed a brief visit to his bedside. Frankie was reported to be 'weak but cheerful'. Cheerful? It was one of the best performances he had given — in his own desperate hour of need he was thinking only of his loved ones.

Barbara Windsor, who lives in a flat close by in Marylebone, slipped in through a back door with a bunch of flowers, found her way to Frankie's room, and gave him a kiss and a word of encouragement. 'I want to go home, dear,' he whispered to her. 'I've had enough of hospitals.'

The last Barbara saw of her old friend was the day he left the clinic. The doctors had done all they could. By chance she was passing by on the opposite pavement just as Frankie emerged through the glass doors, drawn and wan, but smiling bravely for the cameras. He was given a chocolate Easter bunny by a nurse, and a kiss on the cheek to go with it. His own smile never faltered.

Barbara saw it, swallowed back her tears, and walked on.

Frankie went home to die. His one hope was that he could be taken to the pink-walled Somerset cottage in the village of Cross, near Axbridge, where he had spent his happiest hours, walking the fields behind the garden, declaiming poetry to the cows ('They thought I was *mad*!'), relaxing in the tranquil countryside he loved so much.

Sadly, it was not to be.

Frankie's own last supper was on Good Friday, with his sister Betty, just the two of them at his usual round table in the far corner of the Al Gallo d'Oro. Owner Renato Ciarlo remembers him being quieter, more pensive than usual, though he managed a joke or two with the staff. Frankie ate avocado with prawns followed by calves' sweetbreads, with two double vodkas before the meal and a bottle of Frascati to go with it. When he shook hands and said goodbye and went out into the night for the slow stroll home, it was the last time he would be seen in public.

Frankie never admitted that the two weeks after he left hospital were on borrowed time. But Dennis Heymer, who sensed it, was careful to monitor all calls to Edwardes Square. Those who were passed through to Frankie found him putting on a brave face to the world.

June Whitfield, for one. 'I had no idea it would happen so suddenly. The last thing he said to me was: "Let's get together for lunch." I couldn't believe he'd gone when I heard.'

Alfred Marks, for another. On the phone Frankie's voice sounded very weak.

Gently, Alfred asked: 'How are you feeling, Frank?'

'Not too bad, thanks.'

'Let's get together when you feel up to it,' said Alfred.

'Yes, we'll do that,' replied Frankie. 'How about lunch next week?'

'Fine,' said Alfred, and hung up with a sinking feeling in his heart.

'I just knew he had been sent home to die − and he knew it too,' he would say later. 'I just felt most dreadfully sad.'

Frankie died the next day.

EPILOGUE
Titter No More

On that Easter Sunday, 1992, Britain was a sadder place for the twin deaths of two of its comedy giants: Frankie Howerd and Benny Hill. They symbolized the end of an era.

The nineteenth-century essayist Leigh Hunt once wrote: 'The death of a comic actor is felt more than that of a tragedian. He has sympathized more with us in our everyday feelings and has given us more amusement.'

Frankie had passed away in the ambulance rushing him to hospital after he collapsed in his living-room. Over the next few hours the tributes flowed in from far and wide. From fellow comics like Les Dawson ('He was a genius'), Leslie Crowther ('He had honest music hall vulgarity, and took the mickey out of life, love and lust'), Faith Brown ('When he died they broke the mould), Charlie Chester ('He was the perfect lovable amateur who became a great pro') and Ken Dodd ('Another of the comic greats has gone').

And Frankie himself, in the days before his death, summed up his life in one touchingly simple sentence: 'I'm not a good man, but I would like to be . . .'

They buried Frankie Howerd in the little country graveyard of St Gregory's Church in Weare, a mile from his Somerset home. It was a church he had known well. In the rafters above the pulpit is the bizarre sight of a stuffed owl, originally put there to deter bats, but in recent years forming an unblinking audience for Frankie when he would sit alone in a pew rehearsing his lines for his next performance.

The funeral was private, with no flowers by request. Frankie wanted it that way. But the church, with its Norman font and fifteenth-century stained-glass windows, was packed. Betty was supported by Tessa and Dennis. Lee Young had flown in from Australia to say farewell. The Revd George Williams, a retired vicar now responsible for six hamlets in the area, led the service with an address that moved many to tears.

'Frankie loved the simple and the beautiful. He taught us to laugh at ourselves, and not to take ourselves too seriously. We thank God he was able to go on doing that for so long . . .'

Outside in the sunshine, behind the low wall of grey Somerset stone which was Frankie Howerd's last resting place, Cilla and June wept openly for the memory of their friend.

Much of the world beyond that peaceful country churchyard mourned with them the passing of a laughter-maker whose like they would never see again.

A memorial service for him took place on a blustery July afternoon at St Martin-in-the-Fields in London, conducted by the Revd Martin Henwood and filled with Frankie's favourite music. 'Autumn Leaves' and 'Send in the Clowns' were prominent, Frankie's final audience numbered more than eight hundred, and the order of service handed to each of them bore the insignia of a pair of clown masks — one sombre, the other laughing. It was a fitting symbol.

Barry Took was amongst the mourners and had earlier paid his own tribute to Frankie: 'The world has lost one of its dearest and rarest treasures — a true clown.'

Cilla Black, June Whitfield, Barry Cryer, Griff Rhys Jones and Bruce Forsyth also spoke movingly of their old friend, and Cilla's voice was choked with emotion as she said: 'I'm just very proud to have known him. We can talk on a trillion years about dear Frankie's life and never get bored. He was as subtle as an avalanche — and how we loved him!'

Filmography

The Runaway Bus (1954): Director/producer/screenplay: Val
Guest. Photography: Stan Pavey. Cast: Frankie Howerd,
Petula Clark, Margaret Rutherford, Terence Alexander,
George Coulouris.

An Alligator Named Daisy (1955): Director: J. Lee
Thompson. Producer: Raymond Stross. Screenplay: Jack
Davies. Photography: Reginald Wyer. Cast: Donald
Sinden, Stanley Holloway, Jean Carson, Richard Wattis,
Frankie Howerd (guest appearance).

The Ladykillers (1955): Director: Alexander Mackendrick.
Producer: Michael Balcon. Screenplay: William Rose.
Photography: Otto Heller. Cast: Alec Guinness, Cecil
Parker, Peter Sellers, Katie Johnson, Frankie Howerd.

Jumping for Joy (1955): Director: John Paddy Carstairs.
Producer: Raymond Stross. Screenplay: Jack
Davies/Henry Blyth. Photography: Jack Cox.
Cast: Frankie Howerd, Stanley Holloway, A.E. Matthews,
John Hickson.

A Touch of the Sun (1956): Director: Gordon Parry.
Producer: Raymond Stross. Screenplay: Alfred
Shaughnessy. Photography: Arthur Grant. Cast: Frankie
Howerd, Ruby Murray, Dennis Price, Richard Wattis,
Alfie Bass.

Further Up the Creek (1958): Director: Val Guest.
Producer: Henry Halstead. Screenplay: Val Guest/John
Warren/Len Heath. Photography: Gerald Gibbs.
Cast: Frankie Howerd, Shirley Eaton, David Tomlinson,
Thora Hird, Lionel Jeffries.

Watch it Sailor! (1961): Cast: Dennis Price, Liz Fraser,
Graham Stark, Frankie Howerd, Miriam Karlin.

The Fast Lady (1962): Director: Ken Annakin.
Producer: Julian Wintle. Screenplay: Jack Davies/Henry
Blyth. Photography: Reginald Wyer. Cast: Leslie Phillips,

Eric Barker, Stanley Baxter, Dick Emery, Frankie Howerd (guest appearance).

The Cool Mikado (1962): Director/screenplay: Michael Winner. Producer: Harold Baim. Photography: Martin Curtis. Cast: Frankie Howerd, Stubby Kaye, Pete Murray, Tommy Cooper.

The Mouse on the Moon (1963): Director: Richard Lester. Producer: Walter Shenson. Screenplay: Michael Pertwee. Photography: Wilkie Cooper. Cast: Ron Moody, Terry-Thomas, Margaret Rutherford, June Ritchie, Frankie Howerd.

The Great St Trinian's Train Robbery (1966): Director: Frank Launder. Producer: Leslie Gilliat. Screenplay: Frank Launder/Ivor Herbert. Photography: Ken Hodges. Cast: Frankie Howerd, Reg Varney, Stratford Johns, Dora Bryan, Raymond Huntley.

Carry On Doctor (1967): Director: Gerald Thomas. Producer: Peter Rogers. Screenplay: Talbot Rothwell. Photography: Alan Hume. Cast: Frankie Howerd, Sid James, Joan Sims, Kenneth Williams, Barbara Windsor, Hattie Jacques.

Carry On Up the Jungle (1970): Director: Gerald Thomas. Producer: Peter Rogers. Screenplay: Talbot Rothwell. Photography: Ernest Steward. Cast: Frankie Howerd, Joan Sims, Kenneth Connor, Sid James, Charles Hawtrey, Valerie Leon, Terry Scott.

Up Pompeii! (1971): Director: Bob Kellett. Producer: Nat Cohen. Screenplay: Sid Colin. Cast: Frankie Howerd, Julie Ege, Michael Hordern, Barbara Murray, Bernard Bresslaw.

Up the Chastity Belt (1971): Director: Bob Kellett. Producer: Nat Cohen. Cast: Frankie Howerd, Bill Fraser, Anna Quail, Royce Mills.

Up the Front (1972): Director: Bob Kellett. Producer: Nat Cohen. Cast: Frankie Howerd, Zsa Zsa Gabor, Stanley Holloway, Lance Percival.

The House in Nightmare Park (1973): Director: Peter Sykes. Producers: Anglo-EMI. Cast: Frankie Howerd, Ray Milland, Rosalie Crutchley, Kenneth Griffith.

Sergeant Pepper's Lonely Hearts Club Band
(1978): Director: Michael Schultz. Producer: Robert
Stigwood. Music: John Lennon/Paul McCartney.
Cast: Peter Frampton, the Bee Gees, Paul Nicholas,
Frankie Howerd.

Acknowledgements

Photographs courtesy of:
Rex Features
BBC
United Artists
Associated Press
Barratts
Press Association
Thames Television
John Paul
Camera Press
Central Press
London Weekend Television
George Phillips

Sources include:
On the Way I Lost It by Frankie
    Howerd (W.H. Allen)
BBC Written Archive Centre,
    Caversham
Lew Lane Library
British Film Institute
'Three Little Fishes' by Saxie Dowell
    courtesy of Campbell Connelly
    and Co. Ltd., Frith Street,
    London, W1.

Every effort has been made to contact copyright holders, but should any errors or omissions have occurred we will endeavour to correct them in future editions.